A–Z

of

EMBROIDERY
STITCHES

SEARCH PRESS

First published in Great Britain 2014

Search Press Limited
Wellwood, North Farm Road,
Tunbridge Wells, Kent TN2 3DR

First published in Australia by
CB Publications
© CB Publications

ISBN: 978-1-78221-161-7

The Publishers and author can
accept no responsibility for any
consequences arising from the
information, advice or instructions
given in this publication.

Suppliers
If you have difficulty in obtaining
any of the materials and equipment
mentioned in this book, then please
visit the Search Press website for
details of suppliers:
www.searchpress.com

Printed in China

Contents

Hints

Welcome

Embroidery is a way of altering a surface with stitches.

The purpose of this book is simply to show you a variety of stitches. How and where you choose to use them is up to you. Throw the do's and don'ts out the window and experiment by exploring different threads, using needles you feel comfortable with and working on fabric you fall in love with.

What fabric do I use?

The suitability of a fabric for embroidery will be determined by the type of stitching and the intended use of the finished piece. Today we have a wonderful array of fabric available for the embroiderer.

Some embroidery techniques such as counted cross stitch, pulled thread, drawn thread and canvas work, require a certain type of fabric but this doesn't mean that you can't experiment and use others.

Don't feel constrained by traditional ideas of what may be suitable for embroidery.

How do I prepare my fabric?

Fabrics are made from either man-made or natural fibres (or a combination of the two). Occasionally you may encounter problems with shrinking or fraying and you will need to be aware of this when preparing the fabric. Pre-wash fabrics according to the specified care instructions to test for shrinkage and colourfastness.

To prevent the raw edges fraying while stitching the embroidery, neaten all edges of your work.

Avoid using tape to seal the edges as the glue may permanently discolour the fabric and will attract dirt.

Ensure you allow enough fabric around the design for the intended purpose of the finished piece.

How do I care for my embroidery?

Perhaps the biggest threats to your embroidery in the home are insects and light. Protect your stitching from insects (moths and silverfish) by not storing it when it is soiled and by using natural repellents.

These include camphor, cedar or lavender. Take care not to allow the repellent to come into contact with the embroidered piece.

Avoid storing your work in plastic as natural fibres may sweat, causing mildew. Cloth bags made from calico are ideal for storage. Keep your embroidery rolled onto a cardboard tube if storing for long periods of time. Cover the tube with acid-free tissue paper. Roll the embroidery onto the tube with the right side facing out and place it into a cloth bag or roll in another piece of fabric.

Light, particularly direct sunlight, can damage your embroidery by fading both fabric and threads. Try not to place items in direct sunlight or strong artificial light.

When framing your work ask your framer to use conservation glass to screen out harmful UV light.

When things go wrong

Thread manufacturers have changed their dyeing processes to be more environmentally friendly and consequently no longer guarantee their dyes to be colourfast. Some colours may run when you wash your embroidery. If they do, soak the embroidery in cold water and the excess dye should wash out.

Do not use bleach or nappy washing detergents as these are too harsh and may harm your fabric and threads.

Take care when transferring a design with marking pens, transfer sheets or dressmaker's carbon, as some marks can be permanent or difficult to remove and you will have to cover them with embroidery.

If you prick your finger and get blood onto the fabric, chew a piece of sewing thread and use this to dab off the blood. Your saliva removes your own blood marks.

Beginning and ending thread

A stitch is a medium for creating an image. Just as the painter uses a brush and paint, the embroiderer uses a needle and thread.

It is important to secure the thread so that your embroidery stitches don't come undone. This needs to be done when starting a thread and finishing it off. Try to avoid unsightly lumps, large knots and stray threads on the back of your work.

Extra care should be taken with embroideries that require frequent washing, as this can loosen threads. Avoid carrying your thread for long distances on the back of the work, as this may show through on the front (especially if the thread colour is dark). It is better to end off and start again.

Choose your method of beginning and ending according to the type of embroidery you are doing.

Back stitching

A suitable method for most embroidery. Before beginning to stitch, bring the thread to the front in an area to be covered with embroidery. Anchor the thread with two tiny back stitches. Split the first stitch with the second to make the thread very secure. Give it a good tug to test. After working several stitches, trim away any excess thread on the back. Work two tiny back stitches on the wrong side of the fabric in the same manner to end off.

Waste knot

photo 1

photo 2

photo 3

Using a waste knot involves leaving the knot on the surface, a short distance from the start of the embroidery. This method can be used with or without a hoop. Knot the end of the thread. Position the knot on the front approximately 5cm (2") away from where the first stitch will be placed. Bring the thread to the front at the start of the embroidery and begin stitching (photo 1). To end off the waste knot, separate it from the fabric surface and cut it off (photo 2). On the wrong side, thread the tail into the needle and secure under the stitching (photo 3).

Cut off any excess thread.

This method is particularly suited to techniques where there is nowhere to conceal the starting point. These include shadow work, canvas work and petit point.

Weaving

Weaving or taking a tail of thread under the stitching on the back of the work is only suitable for framed embroideries or pieces that do not need washing. Weaving should be used in combination with back stitches to make the tail secure enough for repeated handling.

Leave a 10cm (4") tail of thread dangling on the back of the fabric. After working a small part of the embroidery, re-thread the tail and take two tiny backstitches through the stitching on the back as before. Trim away any excess thread. Working threads can be ended off in the same manner.

Knots

Knots can be used where you have a textured surface as the small lump caused by the knot won't be noticeable. A knot combined with back stitches will be very secure – great for embroidered clothing or table linen or anything that needs to be washed.

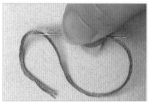

1 **Option 1**. Thread the needle. Hold a short tail of thread along the shaft of the needle with the tail towards the eye.

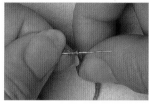

2 Hold the tail and the needle in the left hand. With the right hand, wrap the thread around the point of the needle 2-4 times.

3 Holding the wraps between left thumb and index finger, pull the needle through the wraps. This creates a neat, consistent knot.

4 **Option 2**. Thread the needle. Hold a short tail at right angles to the needle. Wrap and pull thread through wraps as in option 1.

Transferring designs

There are many ways to transfer a design. The method depends on the type of fabric or the particular embroidery technique to be used.

Iron-on transfers leave permanent marks that must be covered by embroidery. Some work more successfully on synthetics than on natural fibres. Transfers are suitable for fabrics with smooth surfaces, such as cotton, polycotton and Doctor's flannel.

Cover a smooth flat object (eg. a wooden board) with aluminium foil, shiny side up. Place the fabric over the board right side up. Pin the transfer design face down onto the fabric ensuring it is correctly positioned. Press firmly with a medium to hot iron, taking care not to move the transfer. Carefully lift a corner to check that the design has been transferred clearly. If not, continue pressing until you have design lines to follow. Care must be taken not to scorch the fabric.

Fabric marking pens are non-permanent and are suitable for fabric with a smooth surface. They are not suitable for framed pieces as the ink may reappear. The lines made with spirit based markers fade and disappear quickly. Lines made with water based markers are removed by dabbing or rinsing in cold water before applying heat. Read the manufacturers' instructions carefully.

Transfer pencils are heat-sensitive pencils that leave permanent lines which will need to be completely covered by embroidery. Draw or trace a mirror image of the finished design onto tracing paper. Iron the design onto the fabric in the same manner as an iron-on transfer.

Chalk based fabric pencils brush or wash off. They are excellent for dark fabrics. Do not use colours on fabrics such as silk, where water marks may be a problem. Trace or draw the design onto the right side of the fabric. As the chalk tends to brush off quickly as you work, tack over the design lines.

Tulle is suitable for any fabric, particularly heavyweight coarse fabrics, such as wool blanketing. Avoid using this method for designs that are particularly intricate. Trace the design onto a piece of tulle with a black permanent marker. Allow to dry thoroughly. Pin the tracing to the right side of the fabric and trace the design with a fabric marker. Ensure the chosen fabric marker is suitable for the fabric.

Direct tracing is suitable for fabrics that are light in colour and relatively sheer. Draw the design onto paper using black ink or a felt tipped pen. Place the design under the fabric on a flat surface. Tape both the fabric and design to the surface and trace the design onto the fabric using a lead pencil or fabric marking pen. Taping to a window or lightbox will make it easier to see the lines.

Templates. This method is useful for transferring simple shapes that are to be repeated several times. First draw or trace the shape onto tracing paper and cut out. Pin the shape to the fabric. Using small stitches and a contrasting thread, tack around the shape close to the edge. Remove the paper. Alternatively, a shape can be cut out in thin card or plastic. Draw around the shape using a chalk pencil or a HB lead pencil.

Tacking is time consuming but gives the most satisfactory results as it leaves no permanent mark. Designs can be altered as the work progresses. This method is excellent for wool blanketing or other fabrics with a rough surface. Using a fine tipped pen, trace the design onto tracing paper. Pin the tracing, design uppermost, onto the right side of the fabric. With contrasting sewing thread, tack along the design lines with small, even, running stitches. Score the tacked lines with the tip of the needle and tear the paper away. Remove the tacking as you work the design.

Dressmaker's carbon comes in several colours and is suitable for fabrics with a smooth surface. The chosen colour will need to show on the background fabric but blend with the embroidery as the lines may be permanent.

Yellow or white are useful for dark coloured heavy-weight fabrics. Place the carbon onto the fabric, waxed side down. Place the design over the carbon.

Hold in place with tape. Draw the design lines using a sharp lead pencil or tracing wheel. Never use typewriter carbon paper.

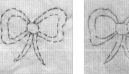

Iron-on transfers   *Direct tracing*   *Templates*   *Tacking*   *Dressmaker's carbon*

Needles

Needles come in a variety of types and sizes. The size of a needle is given as a number. The higher the number, the finer the needle. Ideally, the shaft of the needle should be of a similar thickness to the thread being used. The thread should fill the hole left by the needle when it passes through the fabric.

For more information on needles, see the hints on pages 16 and 19.

Needle	Size (No.)	Suitable for
Chenille A thick needle with a large eye. Similar to a tapestry needle but with a sharp tip. This needle was originally used for tufted chenille yarns.	18-24	Suitable for thick threads such as tapestry wool, crewel wool, six strands of stranded cotton, no.3 and no.5 perle cotton, thick silk and heavy metallic thread. Ideal for ribbon embroidery and wool embroidery.
Crewel (Embroidery) A finer needle with a large, long eye. The large eye makes the needle easier to thread. Sizes 7-9 are ideal for smocking.	9-10	Suitable for fine embroidery using one or two strands of cotton, silk or rayon. Unsuitable for bullion knots as the eye is too wide.
	3-8	Excellent general purpose needles. Use with three to six strands of stranded cotton, silk or rayon and coton á broder (twisted, non-divisible cotton thread), broder médicis (fine wool thread), no.8 and no.12 perle cotton and fine metallic thread.
Sharps A good general purpose needle. The small, round eye provides strength for the needle and prevents excess wear on the thread.	10-12	Suitable for fine embroidery including bullion knots. Use with one or two strands of stranded cotton, silk or rayon. The no.12 is sometimes known as a hand appliqué needle.
	7-9	Use with two or three strands of stranded cotton, silk or rayon. Also suitable for bullion knots.
Straw (Milliner's) These are fabulous for bullions. A straw needle has a tiny eye and a long, fine shaft. Because the eye is no wider than the shaft, they are invaluable for beading and for pulling through the wraps when stitching bullion knots. Traditionally used for work on bonnets and hats.	9-11	Use with one or two strands of stranded cotton, silk or rayon.
	5-8	Use with three or four strands of stranded cotton, silk or rayon.
	1-4	Use with four to six strands of stranded cotton, silk or rayon, no.8 and no.12 perle cotton, coton á broder and metallic threads. Also suitable for Brazilian embroidery using thick, twisted threads.
Tapestry A medium length needle with a thick shaft, a blunt tip and a long eye. The blunt tip parts the fabric threads rather than splitting them.	26-28	Suitable for decorative hem stitching on fine linens, fine counted cross stitch and petit point.
	18-24	Suitable for counted thread embroidery such as cross stitch, blackwork, pulled and drawn thread work and Hardanger. Also suitable for wool embroidery, needleweaving and shadow work.

No.24 Chenille

No.18 Chenille

No.7 Crewel

No.3 Crewel

No.8 Sharp

No.12 Sharp

No.9 Straw (Milliner's)

No.5 Straw (Milliner's)

No.24 Tapestry

No.18 Tapestry

ALGERIAN EYE STITCH

Also known as star eyelet stitch. Algerian eye stitch is a counted thread stitch in which each 'star' consists of eight stitches. The stitches are worked in an anti-clockwise direction and a hole forms in the centre.

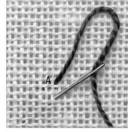

1 Bring the thread to the front at A, 2 fabric threads above the centre hole. Take it to the back through the centre hole.

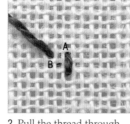

2 Pull the thread through tightly to open up the centre hole. Count 2 fabric threads to the left of A. Bring the thread to the front in the next hole (B).

3 Pull the thread through, then take it to the back through the centre hole to form a diagonal stitch.

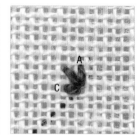

4 Count 2 fabric threads to the left of the centre hole and re-emerge in the next hole (C). Take to the back through the centre hole. Pull through.

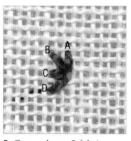

5 Count down 2 fabric threads from C. Re-emerge in the next hole (D) and then take the thread to the back through the centre hole. Pull through.

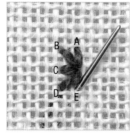

6 Count 2 fabric threads to the right of D and re-emerge in the next hole (E). This is directly below the centre hole.

7 Pull the thread through. Take it to the back through the centre hole and pull through.

8 Count 2 fabric threads to the right of E and bring the thread up through the next hole (F). Take to the back through the centre hole and pull through.

9 Count 2 fabric threads to the right of the centre and re-emerge in the next hole (G). This is directly above F.

10 Take the thread to the back through the centre hole and pull through. Count 2 fabric threads above G and re-emerge in the next hole (H).

11 Take the thread to the back through the centre hole.

12 Pull through and end off on the back of the fabric. **Completed Algerian eye stitch.**

ARROWHEAD STITCH

Arrowhead stitch is often worked as a filling stitch in counted thread and surface embroidery. The arrowhead is made by using two straight stitches at right angles to each other. Here it is worked in a vertical line.

Mark three lines on the fabric to help position the stitches accurately.

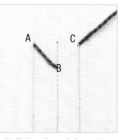

1 Bring the thread to the front at A. Insert the needle at B, below and to the right of A. Re-emerge at C.

2 Pull the thread through to form the first half of the arrowhead stitch.

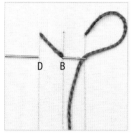

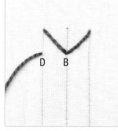

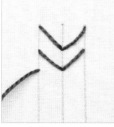

3 Take the needle to the back at B and re-emerge at D.

4 Pull the thread through to complete the first arrowhead stitch. The thread is in position to start the second stitch.

5 Work the second stitch in exactly the same manner, keep-ing the stitches even in length and at right angles to each other.

6 Continue working stitches. To end off, take thread to the back at the tip (B). Secure the thread on the back. **Completed arrowhead stitches**.

BACK STITCH

Back stitch is particularly suited to fine lines and details. It can also be used to form a foundation for combination stitches.

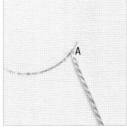

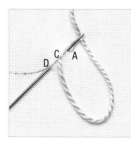

1 Mark a line on the fabric. Bring the thread to the front at A, approx 1.5mm (1/16") from the start of the marked line.

2 Take the needle into the fabric at the starting point (B). Re-emerge approx 1.5mm (1/16") beyond A at C.

3 Pull the thread through to complete the first stitch. Take the needle to the back at A (in exactly the same hole). Re-emerge at D, 3mm (1/8") away.

4 Continue working stitches in the same manner. To end off, take the thread through the hole at the beginning of the previous stitch.

BLANKET STITCH

Blanket stitch was traditionally used to finish the edges of blankets. The basic stitch can be worked with many variations. Here it is shown as an edging stitch for appliqué.

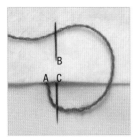

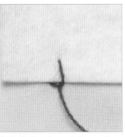

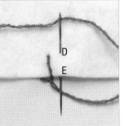

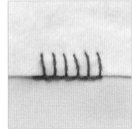

1 Bring the thread to the front at A. Take needle to the back at B and re-emerge at C. The thread is under the tip of the needle.

2 Pull the thread through until the stitch sits snugly against the cut edge of the appliqué fabric but does not distort it.

3 Take the needle to the back at D. Re-emerge at E. Ensure the thread is under the tip of the needle.

4 Continue to work evenly spaced stitches. To end off, take needle to back just over the last loop. **Completed blanket stitch.**

BLANKET STITCH PINWHEEL

Often called blanket pinwheels, these pretty flowers are formed from closely worked blanket stitches radiating from the centre to form a circle. This method of stitching a flower is particularly suitable for working graceful spires of hollyhocks.

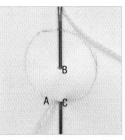

1 Draw a circle and mark the centre. Bring the thread to front at A. Take the needle from B to C (just to the right of A).

2 Place the thread under the needle tip. Begin to pull the thread through, pulling away from the circle.

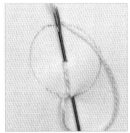

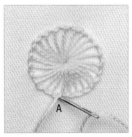

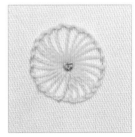

3 Pull until the loop sits on the circle. Again, take the needle from the centre to edge of circle, just right of previous stitch. Ensure thread is under needle.

4 Continue working stitches around the circle, gradually turning the fabric as you work.

5 For last stitch, take needle from centre to A (through same hole). With thread under needle, pull through. To anchor, take needle to back just over loop.

6 Pull the thread through. End off on the back. Work a French knot in the centre to complete the flower. **Completed blanket stitch pinwheel.**

BLANKET STITCH – DOUBLE

This variation of blanket stitch can be worked in one or more thread colours and in curved or straight lines to create distinctive borders. It can also be worked as a filling stitch, adding colour or texture to a shape.

After a row of blanket stitches is worked, the fabric is turned upside down. A second row is then stitched, with the vertical sections of the stitches being placed between those of the first row. Both rows should be of the same height and overlap at the centre.

Drawing two parallel lines will help keep the stitches even.

1 First row. Bring the thread to the front at A. Take the needle from B to C, ensuring the thread lies under the tip of the needle.

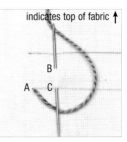

2 Pull the thread towards you until the loop rests gently on the emerging thread.

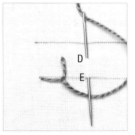

3 Take the needle from D to E. This is the same height as the previous stitch and parallel to it. Ensure the thread is under the tip of the needle.

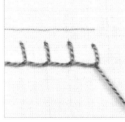

4 Pull the thread through as before. Continue to the end of the row in the same manner.

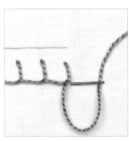

5 To end off, take the thread to the back just over the last loop.

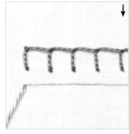

6 Second row. Turn the fabric upside down. Bring thread to front directly below the end of the stitch in the previous row.

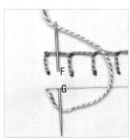

7 Take the needle from F to G in between the vertical stitches of the first row. Ensure the thread is under the tip of the needle.

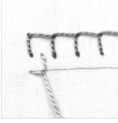

8 Pull the thread towards you until the loop rests gently on the emerging thread.

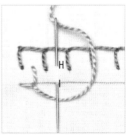

9 Take the needle from H to I between the second and third vertical stitches of the first row. Ensure the thread is under the tip of the needle.

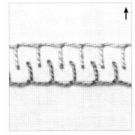

10 Continue to the end of the row, ensuring the stitches are evenly spaced. End off as before. **Completed double blanket stitch.**

BLANKET STITCH – DETACHED

This variation of blanket stitch is worked from left to right on a foundation of straight stitches. The blanket stitches do not go through the fabric.

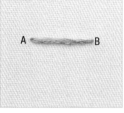

1 Bring the thread to the front at A. Take the needle to the back the required distance away (B). Pull the thread through, forming a straight stitch.

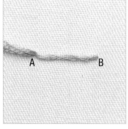

2 Bring the thread to the front in exactly the same position (or as close as possible) to A.

3 Pull the thread through and take it to the back in the same position as the first stitch (B). **Completed foundation.**

4 **Detached blanket stitch.** Bring the needle to the front, just below A. Pull the thread through.

5 Take the needle from top to bottom behind the straight stitches. Do not pierce the fabric.

6 Position the thread under the tip of the needle and begin to pull the thread through.

7 Continue pulling the thread through, pulling it towards you until the stitch wraps snugly around the foundation. **Completed first stitch.**

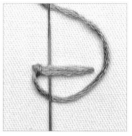

8 Again, take the needle from top to bottom behind the straight stitches without piercing the fabric. Ensure the thread is under the tip of the needle.

9 Pull the thread through ensuring the stitch lies snugly against the first stitch but does not overlap it. **Completed second stitch.**

10 Continue working blanket stitches in the same manner until the straight stitches are completely covered.

11 Take the needle to the back of the fabric just below the end of the straight stitches.

12 Pull the thread through and end off on the back of the fabric. **Completed detached blanket stitch.**

BLANKET STITCH – TWISTED DETACHED

This stitch can be used for raised effects in embroidery. It is stitched in a similar manner to detached blanket stitch.

1 Work the foundation straight stitches and detached blanket stitches following the instruc-tions on page 12. Stop halfway along the foundation.

2 **First twisted stitch.** Take the needle from top to bottom behind the foundation, ensuring it does not pierce the fabric. The thread is under the needle tip.

3 Start to pull the thread towards you until the loop begins to close around the foundation.

4 Take the thread up and away from you.

5 Pull in this direction until the stitch wraps snugly around the foundation. The loop will sit higher than the previous stitches.

6 **Second twisted stitch.** Pull the end of the thread towards you and place the needle under the foundation in the same manner as before.

7 Ensuring the thread is under the tip of the needle begin pulling it towards you.

8 When the loop begins to close around the foundation, take the thread up and away from you as before.

9 Continue pulling up and away from you until the stitch sits snugly around the foundation next to the first twisted stitch.

10 Continue working stitches following steps 6–9, until the foundation has been completely covered.

11 Take the needle to the back of the fabric next to the last loop formed.

12 Pull the thread through and end off on the back of the fabric. **Completed twisted detached blanket stitch.**

BLANKET STITCH – LONG AND SHORT

As the name suggests, long and short blanket stitch has stitches of varying lengths.

Long and short blanket stitch can be used in straight lines or scallops as a decorative edge. When used to fill a shape, the loops define the outline.

Rule two parallel lines on the fabric to help you position the stitches accurately.

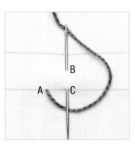

1 Bring the thread to the front at A. Take the needle from B to C. Ensure the thread is under the tip of the needle.

2 Pull thread through (towards you) until the loop rests gently on the emerging thread.

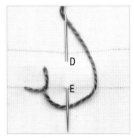

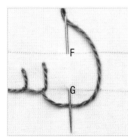

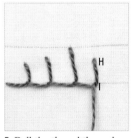

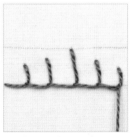

3 Take the needle from D to E. This is parallel to the previous stitch but is slightly higher. Ensure the thread is under the tip of the needle.

4 Pull the thread through as before. Take the needle from F to G.

5 Pull the thread through. Take a stitch from H to I. Pull the thread through.

6 Take another stitch the same height as the first stitch. Pull the thread through.

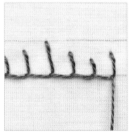

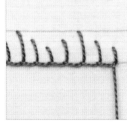

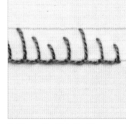

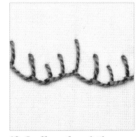

7 Take a sixth stitch the same height as the second stitch. Pull the thread through.

8 While the height of the vertical stitches vary, the loops at the base of the stitches follow the marked outline.

9 To end off, take the thread to the back just over the last loop. **Completed long and short blanket stitch.**

10 **Scalloped variation.** Mark the shape onto the fabric. Work the stitches in the same manner as steps 1–6 but the needle re-emerges on a scalloped outline.

BLANKET STITCH – LOOPED

Looped blanket stitch is sometimes worked in a circle to form a blanket stitch rose. Loops need to be kept even and consistent in size. We used two different colours of thread for photographic purposes only.

1 Draw two circles, 1cm (⅜") and 1.5cm (⅝") in diameter on the fabric. Bring the needle to the front at A on the inner circle.

2 Take the needle to the back at B and re-emerge at C. Ensure the thread is under the tip of the needle.

3 Gently pull the thread through, leaving enough thread to make a loop that just touches the outer circle.

4 Hold the thread to the left with the thumb. Take the needle to the back at D and to the front at E. Make a second loop the same size as the first.

5 Continue working around the circle. Make stitches as close as possible and keep loops even in size. Turn work as necessary.

6 To complete the circle, take the needle to the back behind the first loop.

7 Completed first circle.

8 Bring the needle to the front at F, just inside the previous circle of stitches. Take the needle to the back at G and out at H (on inner circle).

9 Continue working a second circle inside the first circle of loops in the same manner.

10 Completed second circle.

11 Work a third circle inside the second circle of loops in the same manner. **Completed third circle.**

12 Continue working smaller and smaller circles until the fabric is covered. Place a French knot in the centre. **Completed looped blanket stitch rose.**

BLANKET STITCH – SCALLOPS

Blanket stitch is a versatile stitch used in many types of embroidery. Here it not only forms a decorative finish, but also neatens the raw edge of the fabric to prevent fraying. Work the stitches close together so no background fabric shows through.

Mark double lines onto the right side of the fabric for the scallops.

Use these lines as a guide for the length of the stitches but not for the direction in which the stitches lie.

When working on fine fabrics, tack fabric stabilizer behind the scallops for stability.

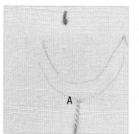

1 Using a waste knot, bring the thread to the front at A on the outside line of the deepest point of one scallop.

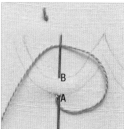

2 Take the needle from B to A, keeping the stitch at right angles to the outer line.

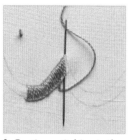

3 Continue stitching in the same manner. Ensure that only one stitch sits at the very peak of each scallop and remains at right angles to the outer line.

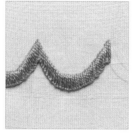

4 Finish off by taking the thread to the back just over the last loop. Cut off the waste knot and secure the tail under the threads on the back.

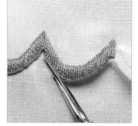

5 **Completed scallops.** Cut away the excess fabric along the outer edge of the scallops. Take care not to cut the stitching.

wrong side of fabric

6 After working the scallops, carefully cut away the excess stabilizer along the inner edge of the scallops.

Hints on threading needles

1 Ensure that the end of the thread has been cut cleanly – on an angle may help. Any stray fibres can push the thread away from the needle when you try to thread it.

2 Moisten the end of the thread and flatten it between your fingers. The eye of the needle is an elongated shape, not round, so you need to make the thread fit the eye. After threading, cut the wet piece off.

3 If you are having real difficulty, try a size larger needle.

4 Are you using the right end of the thread? Make sure you are threading with the grain running down the thread. The wrong end will 'frizz up' as you try to push it through the eye.

5 When threading wools, try folding the end of the thread around the needle. Pinch it tightly and slide it off the needle. Push the folded piece through the eye.

BRAID STITCH

Braid stitch is worked from right to left and gives a textured border with a braided appearance.

This stitch is suitable for curves or straight lines. Marking parallel lines will help to keep your stitches even. To achieve a textured look, twisted threads such as perle cottons should be used, rather than stranded cottons. The stitches are best worked small and close together. Our stitches are spaced out for photographic purposes only.

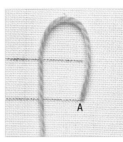

1 Bring the thread to the front at A on the lower line. Loop the thread to the left of A.

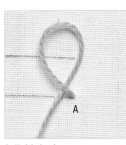

2 Fold the loop over so the working thread crosses behind the emerging thread.

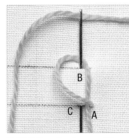

3 Holding the loop with your thumb, insert needle through loop at B on upper line (thumb not shown). Re-emerge at C, directly below on the lower line.

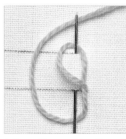

4 Loop the working thread from right to left, taking it under the tip of the needle.

5 Pull the loop tightly around the needle.

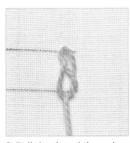

6 Pull the thread through in a downward motion.

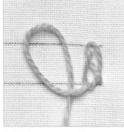

7 Make a second loop following steps 1 and 2.

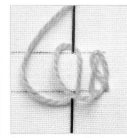

8 Insert the needle through the loop and into the fabric on the upper line. Re-emerge on lower line. Loop the thread to the left under the needle as before.

9 Pull the thread through to complete the second stitch.

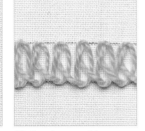

10 Continue working stitches in the same manner. **Completed braid stitch.**

BULLION KNOT

A bullion knot is a raised stitch of twisted thread lying on top of the fabric.

There is no formula for the perfect bullion. Practise making bullions using different threads varying the length of the stitch, the number of threads and number of wraps.

Understanding how a stitch is formed helps to alleviate problems. We used a no.8 straw needle and two strands of thread.

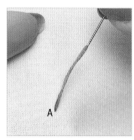

1 Bring the needle to the front at A. Pull the thread through. The distance between A and B will be the required length of the finished bullion knot.

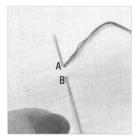

2 Take the needle to the back at B and re-emerge at A, taking care not to split the thread. The thread is to the right of needle.

3 With your left thumb over the eye of the needle, raise the point of the needle in the air. Wind thread clockwise around needle.

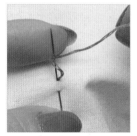

4 With left index finger behind the needle, pull the first wrap firmly down onto the fabric.

5 Work 4 more wraps evenly around the shaft of the needle. You will now have 5 wraps.

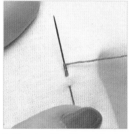

6 Keeping the thread taut (to maintain tension on the wraps), pack the wraps of thread evenly down the needle onto the fabric.

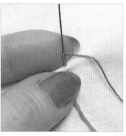

7 Keeping the tension on the wraps with the left index finger, begin to ease the needle through the fabric and the wraps.

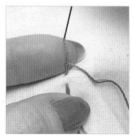

8 Continuing to keep the pressure on the wraps with the index finger, pull the needle and thread through the wraps.

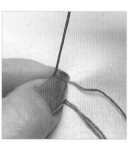

9 Now place the index finger and the thumb on the wraps. Holding firmly, continue to pull the thread away from you and through the wraps.

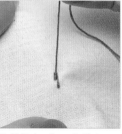

10 Pull the thread all the way through, tugging the wraps **away** from you. This helps to ensure a tight, even knot.

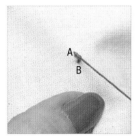  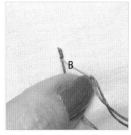 

11 Now pull the thread firmly **towards** you (towards position B). Keep the thread taut. The knot now sits between A and B.

12 To ensure all the wraps are even, gently stroke and manipu-late them with the needle. Keep tension tight and take your time.

13 Anchor the knot by taking the needle to the back at B. **Completed bullion knot.**

Rosebud formed with two pink bullion knots, a fly stitch calyx and a detached chain leaf.

Hints on creating perfect bullion knots

Type of Needle

There are several advantages to using a straw (milliner's) needle for bullions.

1 The shaft. Unlike most other needles, the diameter of the shaft is the same from the top of the needle to where it starts tapering to a point. The wraps will therefore maintain an even tension when the needle and thread are pulled through.

2 Length. The straw needle has a longer shaft than most other needles. This length is necessary to hold the varying number of wraps required.

Number of Strands

The number of strands is determined by the thickness of the stitch required – the greater number of strands used, the thicker the stitch.

Size of Bullion

The distance between A and B is the length of the bullion. You will need enough wraps to cover this distance.

For a curved bullion stitch, more wraps will be added. If 5 wraps make a straight bullion, you will need at least 3 - 4 more for a curved bullion, depending on the curve required.

Problem Solving

The wraps are not even.

This is caused by the tension on the wraps not being maintained. Ensure the first and last wraps are even. Don't be afraid to 'play' with the wraps before anchoring the bullion knot. To achieve an even tension, lift the bullion up from the fabric and run the shaft of the needle under the wraps, pulling the thread at the same time to tighten the wraps.

The needle does not pull through the wraps.

This is due to the wraps being too tight around the needle. Slightly twist the needle in the opposite direction to the wraps on the needle. This will loosen the wraps and allow the needle to be pulled through.

BULLION KNOT – ROSE WITH BULLION CENTRE

This classic bullion rose is created from two rounds of petals surrounding a pair of bullion knots. The inner round of petals has three bullion knots and the outer round, six. We used a no.8 straw needle and two strands of thread.

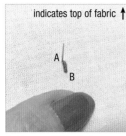

indicates top of fabric ↑

1 Centre. With darkest thread shade, stitch a bullion knot fol-lowing steps on pages 18 & 19. For second bullion, bring needle to front again very close to A.

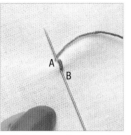

2 Pull the needle through the fabric. Insert at B, re-emerging at A again. The thread is to the right of the needle.

3 Wrap the thread clockwise around the needle 5 times, holding the thread taut. Pack the wraps evenly down the needle onto the fabric.

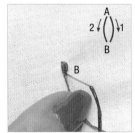

4 Anchor the second bullion by taking the needle to the back at B.

5 Completed centre bullions of rose.

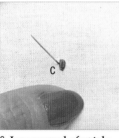

6 Inner round of petals. Change to a lighter thread shade. To work the first petal of the inner round, bring the needle to the front at C.

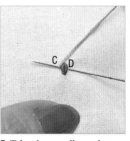

7 Take the needle to the back at D and re-emerge at C. The thread is still to the right of the needle and held taut.

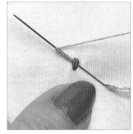

8 Maintaining thread tension, wrap the thread around the needle 9 times. Pack the wraps evenly down the needle.

9 Pull the thread through, keeping it taut and settling the knot in position around the tip of the centre bullions.

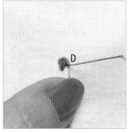

10 After adjusting the knot to your satisfaction, anchor it at D.

11 Completed first petal of the inner round. The petal lies snugly curled around the centre bullions.

12 Bring the needle to the front at E.

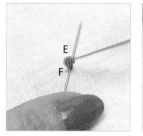

13 Take the needle to the back at F and re-emerge at E.

14 Wrap the thread clockwise around the needle 9 times, holding it taut to maintain tension on the wraps.

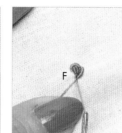

15 Anchor this petal by taking the needle to the back at F.
Completed second petal of the inner round.

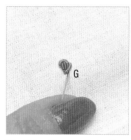

16 Bring the needle to the front at G.

17 Rotate the fabric upside down. Take the needle to the back at H and re-emerge at G.

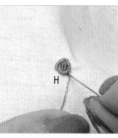

18 Wrap thread around needle 9 times. Pull the thread through. Anchor this petal by taking the needle to the back at H.

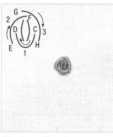

19 **Completed inner round.**

20 **Outer round of petals.**
Change thread colour to the lightest shade. Bring the needle to the front at I. Rotate the fabric slightly as necessary.

21 Take the needle to the back at J and re-emerge at I.

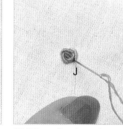

22 Wrap the thread around the needle 10 times, holding it taut. Pull thread through. Anchor this petal by taking the needle to the back at J.

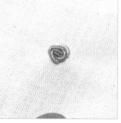

23 **Completed first petal of the outer round.**

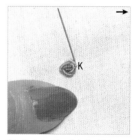

24 Rotate the fabric. Bring the needle to the front at K.

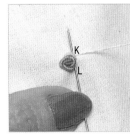

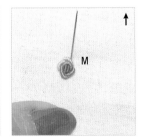

25 Take the needle to the back at L and re-emerge at K.

26 Wrap thread around needle 10 times, holding taut to maintain tension. Pull the thread through. Anchor this petal by taking the needle to the back at L.

27 Completed second petal of the outer round.

28 Rotate the fabric. Bring the needle to the front at M.

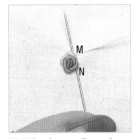

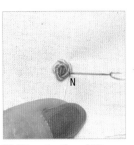

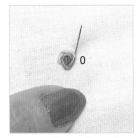

29 Take the needle to the back at N and re-emerge at M.

30 Wrap the thread 10 times and pull through. Anchor this petal by taking the needle to the back at N.

31 Completed third petal of the outer round.

32 Bring the needle to the front at O.

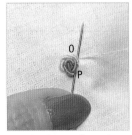

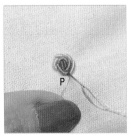

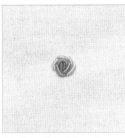

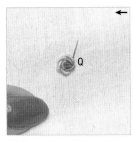

33 Take the needle to the back at P and re-emerge at O.

34 Wrap the thread 10 times and pull through. Anchor this petal by taking the needle to the back at P.

35 Completed fourth petal of the outer round.

36 Rotate the fabric and bring the needle to the front at Q.

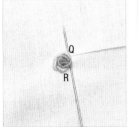

37 Take the needle to the back at R and re-emerge at Q.

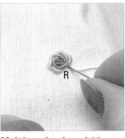

38 Wrap the thread 10 times and pull through. Anchor this petal by taking the needle to the back at R.

39 **Completed fifth petal of the outer round.**

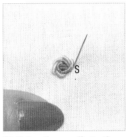

40 Bring the needle to the front at S.

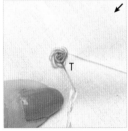

41 Rotate fabric slightly. Take needle to the back at T (tucked inside first bullion of this round).

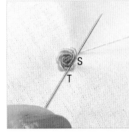

42 The needle re-emerges at S.

43 Wrap the thread 10 times and pull through. Anchor this petal at T (inside the petal that goes from I–J).

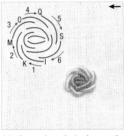

44 **Completed sixth petal of the outer round.** You have now completed your rose. Well done!

Variations

Bullion knot rose in three shades with detached chain leaves.

Bullion knot roses with satin stitch centres and detached chain leaves.

Bullion knot roses and buds. The buds are stitched with a fly stitch for the calyx.

Bullion knot rose in three colours with French knot forget-me-nots and detached chain leaves.

BULLION KNOT – THE SUSAN O'CONNOR ROSE

 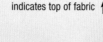This variation uses three shades of pink thread and begins with a bullion loop in the centre. Susan uses two strands of silk thread.

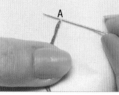
indicates top of fabric ↑

A

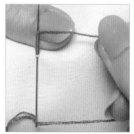

1 Centre. Begin with the dark-est shade. Anchor the thread and bring it to the front at A. Take a tiny stitch very close to A. Leave the needle in the fabric.

2 Place your thumb under the tip of the needle to raise it off the fabric. Take the thread under the needle.

3 Rotate the fabric so that the needle faces upwards and away from you. Wrap the thread once clockwise around the shaft of the needle.

4 Wrap the thread evenly around the needle 9 more times. Use your thumb and forefinger to keep the wraps on the needle. Ensure wraps sit close together.

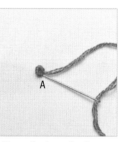

B

5 Placing your left thumb on the wraps to hold them firmly, begin to ease the eye of the needle through the wraps.

6 Keeping your thumb on the wraps, continue pulling until the two ends of the loop come together and the wraps are tight (thumb not shown).

7 Press the loop firmly with your thumb so it lies flat on the fabric. Take the needle to the back at A. End off on the back with a tiny back stitch.

8 Inner petals. Rotate fabric. Change to a lighter shade and secure the thread on the back. Bring needle to front at B, halfway along one side of loop.

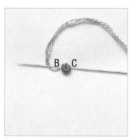

B C

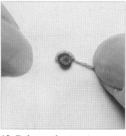

9 Take the needle from C to B, leaving it in the fabric.

10 Wrap the thread clockwise around the needle 10 times.

11 With your thumb over the wraps, pull the needle through the wraps. Pull thread tightly until the fabric forms a pleat (thumb not shown).

12 Release the tension on the working thread. Stretch the fabric flat again. This will cause the stitch to fall into position. Each inner petal forms a half-circle.

"This is a lazy man's rose. I find it easier to stitch a rose using the same number of wraps in every bullion rather than the usual method of increasing the wraps in each successive round of bullion knot petals." Susan O'Connor

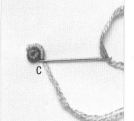

13 Take the needle to the back at C.

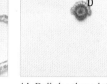

14 Pull the thread through and re-emerge at D.

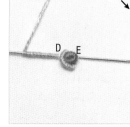

15 Rotate the fabric. Take the needle from E to D. Wrap the thread around the needle 10 times.

16 Pull the thread through. Take the needle to the back at E to complete the second petal. Bring the thread to the front at F.

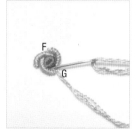

17 Take the needle from G (between the centre and first petal) to F. Wrap 10 times. Take the needle to the back at G forming a bullion from G to F.

18 End off on the back. Rotate the fabric. Change to a lighter shade and bring the thread to the front at H.

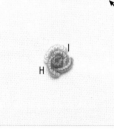

19 Rotate the fabric. Take the needle from I to H and wrap the thread 10 times. Complete the bullion knot as before.

20 Bring the needle to the front at J. Work a 10 wrap bullion knot from K to J.

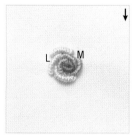

21 Bring the needle to the front at L. Rotate the fabric. Work a 10 wrap bullion knot from M to L.

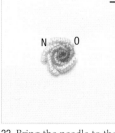

22 Bring the needle to the front at N. Rotate the fabric. Work a 10 wrap bullion knot from O to N.

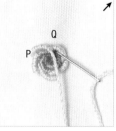

23 Bring the needle to the front at P. Rotate the fabric. Work a 10 wrap bullion knot from Q to P. Q is just inside the first bullion knot of this round.

24 Pull the thread through and end off on back of the fabric. **Completed bullion rose.**

BULLION KNOT – ROSEBUDS

Different types of rosebuds may be formed by varying the thread colours and differing the number of knots and wraps.

Small rosebud

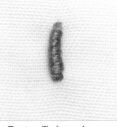   

1 Centre. To form the centre, stitch a 6 wrap bullion knot using the darker thread.

2 Outer petals. Change to a lighter thread. Starting at the base of the centre knot, work a second 6 wrap bullion just to the right of the centre knot.

3 Again, starting at the base, work a third 6 wrap knot on the opposite side.

4 Calyx. Add a green fly stitch for the calyx. Place the tips of the fly stitch halfway along, and very close to, the outer petals. Use a long anchoring stitch.

Medium rosebud

1 Centre. Work a 6 wrap bul-lion knot in the darkest shade. Stitch a second knot alongside, but slightly higher than the first.

2 Outer petals. Change colour. Starting at base of right hand centre petal, work a 10 wrap bullion knot next to left petal.

3 Change colour. Starting just below and to the left of the previous petal, work a second 10 wrap bullion on the right hand side.

4 Calyx. Change colour. Stitch a 6 wrap bullion on either side of the petals, starting in the same hole. Add a third bullion knot for the stem.

Large rosebud

1 Centre. Work a single 6 wrap bullion knot for the centre in the darkest shade of thread.

2 Inner petals. Change colour. Add a bullion on the right hand side, starting level with base of centre knot. Stitch a second bullion, starting just below previous knot on a curve around left side.

3 Outer petals. Change colour. Work 3 bullion knots, starting at base. Place first knot to the right. The next two knots alternate from left to right, starting each just below previous one.

4 Calyx. Change to green thread. Stitch the calyx in the same manner as on the medium rosebud. The centre knot finish-es at the base of the third petal.

BULLION KNOT – ROSE WITH PADDED SATIN CENTRE

This rose has a padded satin stitch centre and is surrounded by bullion petals. It looks particularly beautiful when stitched with one or two strands of silk thread.

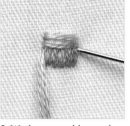

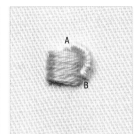

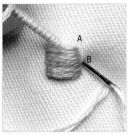

1 **Centre.** Mark a square with sides measuring approximately 5mm (¼") onto the fabric. Fill the square with vertical satin stitches.

2 Work a second layer of satin stitches in a horizontal direction over the first.

3 **Petals** Bring needle to the front at A, halfway across top of padded centre. Take the needle from B to A. Wrap thread around needle 8–10 times.

4 Pull the thread through. Take the needle to the back at B to anchor the bullion knot. **First completed petal.**

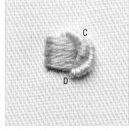

5 Bring the needle to the front at C, approximately halfway along the first bullion knot. Take the needle from D to C and work a second bullion knot.

6 Work three more bullion knots in the same manner, turning the fabric slightly for each bullion.

To work the last petal, bring the needle to the front at E. Take it to the back at F, tucked in between first petal and satin stitch centre. Re-emerge at E.

8 Complete the bullion knot (F–E) in the same manner as before. **Completed bullion rose with padded satin stitch centre**.

Hints on silk thread

A wide range of silk threads from flat, untwisted filament silks to heavy, twisted buttonhole threads are available. Choose the thread suitable for the finish you wish to achieve.

Many silk threads are not washable because of their inability to hold dyed colour. You therefore need to decide whether silk is an appropriate thread for your project. If the silk is not labelled 'colourfast' wash the thread first.

Store your threads away from direct light, especially sunlight, as the colours will fade quickly. The same applies for finished pieces of work.

For large projects, buy threads from the same dye lot to avoid discrepancies in the colour.

Silk is an incredibly strong fibre. Unlike cotton, it does not wear easily and break suddenly.

Silk embroidery is enhanced by being ironed lightly on the back. Steam increases the thread sheen.

BULLION KNOT – BEARS

These little bears are created using four strands of silk thread. Draw a small circle for the head and an oval for the body. Mark the ends of the arms and legs with a dot.

1 Body. Secure the thread on the back of the fabric. Bring to the front at the top of the bear's body. Work a 10 wrap bullion knot to form centre of the body.

2 Work two, 11 wrap bullion knots, one on either side of the first bullion.

3 Work two, 7 wrap bullions, one on either side, to complete the body. Note: these stitches are worked from the top of the body to two-thirds of the length.

4 Head. Work a 6 wrap bullion knot across the top of the body.

5 Work two, 7 wrap bullion knots and then a 6 wrap bullion knot to complete the head. Add an 8 wrap bullion loop on either side of the head for the ears.

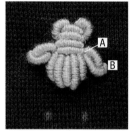

6 Arms. Work a 10 wrap bullion for upper arm. Bring needle to front at A. Stitch an 11 wrap knot from B to A directly under the first. Repeat for second arm.

7 Legs. Work a 10 wrap bullion knot for the outer leg. This knot extends from the lower end of the body's outer bullion knot.

8 Stitch an 11 wrap bullion for the inner leg. A 7 wrap bullion forms each foot. This knot curls around the lower ends of the two bullion knots in the leg.

9 Face. Using 1 strand of black, work 3 straight stitches vertically over the third bullion knot for the nose. Starting just under the nose, work a diagonal stitch to the left into the lower bullion.

10 From the same point at base of nose, work a second diagonal stitch to the right. Work 2 French knots for the eyes on the second bullion knot from the top.

11 Bow tie. (boy). Using 1 strand, take thread to back, leaving a 15cm (6") tail on front. Bring to front close to entry point. Tie threads into bow. Trim tails to 5mm (¼"). Stitch to secure bow.

12 Bow (girl). The bow on the girl bear's head is worked in the same manner as the boy bear's bow tie.

BULLION KNOT – BOW

This dainty bullion knot bow is formed with bullion knot loops for the bow and a single long bullion for each tie.

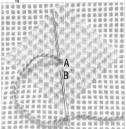

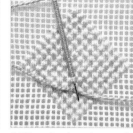

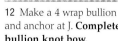

1 Bow loops. Secure the thread on the back. Bring it to the front at A to start the left loop. Take a tiny stitch from B to A.

2 Wrap the thread around the needle 25 times.

3 Hold the wraps between the thumb and forefinger while carefully easing them over the eye of the needle.

4 Keeping thumb on wraps, pull the needle and thread through firmly until a loop is formed (thumb not shown).

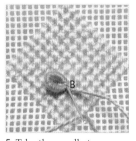

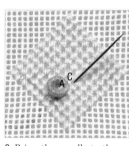

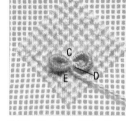

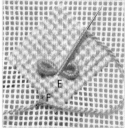
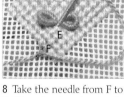

5 Take the needle to the back at B to anchor the loop. **Completed first loop.**

6 Bring the needle to the front at C, very close to A.

7 Working from D to C, repeat steps 1-5 to form the right hand loop. **Completed bow loops. Bow ties.** Bring the thread to the front at E (just below B).

8 Take the needle from F to E. Wrap the thread around the needle 18 times.

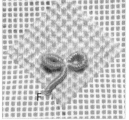

9 Carefully pull the thread through the wraps and anchor the knot at F. **Completed left tie.**

10 Work an 18 wrap bullion from G to H (G is just below D). **Completed ties.**

11 Bow knot. Bring the thread to the front at I, between E and G. Take the needle from J to I.

12 Make a 4 wrap bullion and anchor at J. **Completed bullion knot bow.**

29

BULLION KNOT – DETACHED CHAIN COMBINATION

This combination stitch is ideal for creating flowers. It is worked by beginning a detached chain stitch from the centre and anchoring it with a bullion knot. To stitch a flower, draw two circles on the fabric to use as a guide.

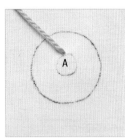

1 Bring the thread to the front at A on the inner circle.

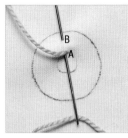

2 Take the needle to the back just to the right of A and out at B, approx halfway between the two circles. The thread is to the left of the needle.

3 Take the thread from left to right under the tip of the needle, pulling it firmly to the right.

4 Wrap the thread clockwise around the needle.

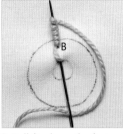

5 Pull firmly, so the first wrap lies snugly against the fabric at B. Wrap thread around needle the required number of times, keeping wraps close together.

6 Place the left thumb over the wraps to hold firmly. Begin to ease the eye of the needle through the wraps.

7 Keeping the thumb and fore-finger on the wraps, pull thread through (thumb not shown).

8 Pull the thread firmly all the way through, until a tight bullion is formed at the end of the detached chain.

9 Take the needle to the back at C, just past the outer circle, to anchor the stitch.

10 **Completed first petal of bullion knot-detached chain combination flower.**

11 Stitch the required number of petals, working from inner to outer circle.

12 **Completed bullion knot-detached chain combination flowers.**

BUTTONHOLE STITCH

True buttonhole stitch forms a row of 'purls' (knots) along the cut edge. When worked as a buttonhole (as shown) or in cutwork, this adds strength to the cut edge. Mark the buttonhole on the fabric. Cut the opening.

↑ indicates top of fabric

1 Buttonhole stitch. Take the needle through the opening and re-emerge on lower line. Pull through leaving a 2cm (¾") tail.

2 Take the needle through the opening and re-emerge on the lower line next to the first stitch. Wrap thread clockwise behind eye and then tip of needle.

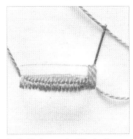

3 Begin to pull the thread through, pulling towards you and then upwards away from the opening.

4 Continue to pull the thread upwards so the loop slips along the stitch towards the opening. A 'purl' forms on the cut edge of the opening.

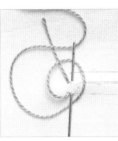

5 Take the needle through the opening and re-emerge next to the previous stitch. Wrap the thread clockwise around the needle as before.

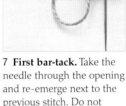

6 Pull through until the 'purl' sits at the cut edge. Continue until you reach the end of the opening. Keep the stitches as close as possible.

7 First bar-tack. Take the needle through the opening and re-emerge next to the previous stitch. Do not wrap the thread around the needle.

8 Pull through. Work three 4mm (³⁄₁₆") long stitches across the end. Take the needle to the back at the upper edge, next to the last stitch.

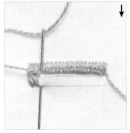

9 Turn the fabric upside down. Bring the thread to the front through the opening. Take the needle back through the opening and re-emerge on lower line.

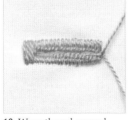

10 Wrap thread around needle as before. Pull through. Continue working stitches to the end.

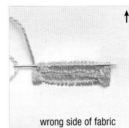

wrong side of fabric

11 Make a bar-tack as in step 8. Finish with needle at the back. Turn fabric to wrong side. Take needle behind the stitches only. Do not go through the fabric.

12 Pull through and trim thread. Secure the tail at the beginning in the same manner. **Completed buttonhole.**

CAST-ON STITCH – ROSE

Cast-on stitch is used in Brazilian embroidery, which makes extensive use of raised stitches. Each cast-on stitch consists of a number of loops cast onto the needle and then anchored to the fabric.

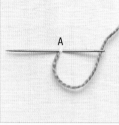

1 **Centre.** Using the darkest thread shade, bring it to the front at A. Take a tiny stitch close to A and leave the needle in the fabric.

2 With your finger facing you, place the emerging thread over your left index finger.

3 Rotate your finger towards you. Keep the thread taut and looped over your index finger.

4 Take the tip of your finger under the working thread and then under the emerging thread, wrapping a loop around your finger.

5 Keeping the tension on the thread, place your finger tip on the point of the needle.

6 Slip the loop off your finger and onto the needle.

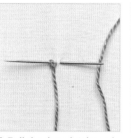

7 Pull the thread tight and slip the loop down the needle onto the fabric. **First cast-on**.

8 Work a second cast-on in the same manner, positioning it on the needle alongside the first.

9 Work 10 more cast-ons onto the needle.

10 Hold the cast-ons in your left hand. With your right hand, pull the needle and thread through the stitches.

11 To anchor the stitch, take the needle to the back at B, close to where the needle last emerged.

12 Pull the thread through. Pull firmly but do not let the fabric pucker. End off the thread. **Completed centre.**

In our rose, the centre is one cast-on stitch. Five cast-on stitches form the first round of petals and seven cast-on stitches form the second round. The fabric is rotated as each stitch is worked. We recommend a no.3 straw (milliner's) needle and Brazilian embroidery thread such as Lola.

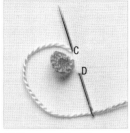

13 Inner petals. Change to a lighter shade. Bring needle to front at C. Insert needle at D, approx 6mm (¼") from C. Re-emerge at C. Do not pull through.

14 Follow steps 2–8 and then work 14 more cast-ons.

15 Holding the cast-ons with your left hand, pull the needle and thread through them with your right hand.

16 Anchor the stitch at D in the same manner as before.

17 Bring the needle to the front at E. Take it from F to E and leave the needle in the fabric.

18 Work a second stitch with 16 cast-ons in the same manner as before. Work three more stitches, each with 16 cast-ons, to complete the inner round.

19 Outer petals. Change to a lighter shade. Bring the needle to the front just underneath one petal of the inner round.

20 Work 7 overlapping stitches in the same manner, with 19 cast-ons in each stitch, to complete the outer round of petals. **Completed cast-on stitch rose.**

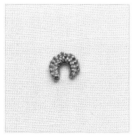

21 Leaves. Stitch the outer leaf first, using 14 cast-ons. The two points where the needle pierces the fabric are placed approx 4mm (³⁄₁₆") apart.

22 Bring the thread to the front, between the ends of the pre-vious stitch. Take the needle through the fabric just beyond the first leaf and re-emerge at G.

23 Stitch the inner leaf using 12 cast-ons.

24 Work two sets of leaves alongside the rose.

CHAIN STITCH

Chain stitch is one of the most versatile of all the basic embroidery stitches. It can be used as a broad textured outline or worked in closely positioned rows to fill a shape. Take care not to pull the loops too tight.

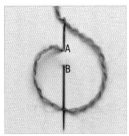

1 Bring the thread to the front at A. Take the needle to the back through the same hole. Re-emerge at B, ensuring the thread is under the tip of the needle.

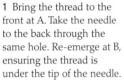

2 Pull the thread through until the loop begins to tighten around the thread.

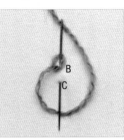

3 Continue pulling until the loop rests gently on the emerg-ing thread. Take the needle from B to C to complete the first stitch and to begin the second stitch.

4 Continue stitching in the same manner for the required distance. To secure the last stitch, take the needle to the back just below the last loop.

CHAIN STITCH – TWISTED

This is a simple variation of basic chain stitch. The added twist gives the stitch a textured, rope-like effect. Each stitch can vary in length and will achieve a different look depending on the thread used.

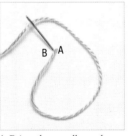

1 Bring the needle to the front at A. Take it to the back at B. Form a loop to the left with the emerging thread.

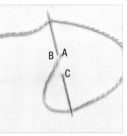

2 Bring the needle to the front at C (below A). The needle is slightly angled towards the right and the thread is positioned under the needle tip.

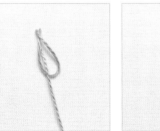

3 Begin to pull the thread through gently until the loop begins to tighten.

4 Continue pulling the thread through until the loop rests on the emerging thread. **Completed first twisted chain stitch.**

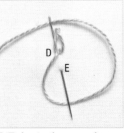

5 To begin the second stitch, take the needle from D (just to the left of the previous loop) to E. Position the thread under the needle tip.

6 Continue for the required distance. To end off, take the needle to the back just below the last loop.

CHAIN STITCH – ALTERNATING

Also known as magic chain or chequered chain stitch. This ingenious stitch is worked with two different coloured threads in the needle at the same time. Work the stitches downwards along a line.

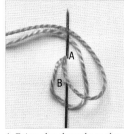

1 Bring the threads to the front at A. Insert the needle into the fabric from A to B. Ensure one thread is under the needle tip and the other is over the needle.

2 Pull the threads through, pulling downwards.

3 Insert the needle into the fabric from B to C. Swap thread colours. Ensure that the second thread is under the needle tip and the first is over the needle.

4 Pull the thread through. Continue working stitches, alternating the thread colour under the tip of the needle. **Completed alternating chain stitch.**

CHAIN STITCH – WHIPPED

Whipped chain stitch is a combination stitch. A line of chain stitch forms the foundation row. Each chain stitch is then whipped with a new thread. The whipping thread does not go through the fabric except at the beginning and end. For added interest, contrasting thread may be used for the whipping. Work the stitches downwards.

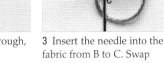

1 **Foundation row.** Mark your design line onto the fabric. Work a row of chain stitch following the line.

2 **Whipping.** Using a second thread, bring the needle to the front at A, just to the left and half- way along the first chain stitch.

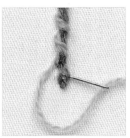

3 Pull the thread through. Take the needle from right to left under the second stitch. It does not go through the fabric.

4 Pull the thread through. **First whipped stitch.**

5 Continue taking the thread from the right to the left under each stitch. To end off, take the needle to the back under the last chain stitch.

6 **Completed whipped chain stitch.**

CHAIN STITCH – INTERLACED

This stitch can be worked with contrasting threads to give it a braid-like appearance. The lacing thread hugs the foundation stitches but does not go through the fabric except at the beginning and end. Work stitches downwards.

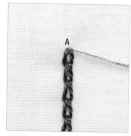

1 Work a line of chain stitch as a foundation. **Interlacing the first side.** Using a new thread, bring it to the front at the top of the line of chain stitch (A).

2 Slide the needle from the right to the left under the right hand side only of the second chain stitch.

3 Pull the thread through. Slide the needle from left to right under the right hand side of the first chain stitch and the adjacent lacing thread.

4 Pull the thread through. Slide the needle from right to left under the right hand side of the third chain stitch.

5 Pull the thread through. Slide the needle from left to right under the previous chain stitch and lacing thread.

6 Continue to the end of the line following steps 4–5. To end off, take the needle to the back at the end of the last chain stitch.

7 Secure the thread on the back. **Completed first side of interlacing.**

8 **Second side.** Using a new thread, bring the thread to the front at A.

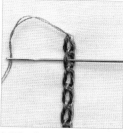

9 Take the needle from the left to the right under the left hand side of the second chain stitch.

10 Pull the thread through. Take the needle from right to left under the first chain stitch and the adjacent lacing thread.

11 Pull the thread through. Continue in this manner, work-ing a mirror image of the first side of interlacing.

12 End off the second side in the same manner as the first. **Completed interlaced chain stitch.**

CHAIN STITCH – OPEN

This chain stitch variation gives a ladder-like effect. It is also known as Roman chain or square chain stitch. Work the stitches downwards. Mark two parallel lines onto the fabric to help keep the stitches even.

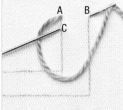

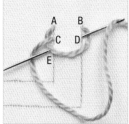

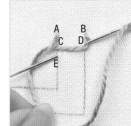

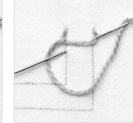

1 Bring the thread to the front at A. Take it to the back at B (level with A), on the right hand line. Re-emerge at C and loop thread under needle tip.

2 Begin to pull thread through. As the loop tightens, take needle to back at D (inside loop). Re-emerge at E (beyond loop). The thread is under the needle tip.

3 Pick up the working thread. Gently pull towards you until the looped stitch sits snugly around the thread and needle. **Completed first stitch.**

4 **Second stitch.** Loop the thread under the needle.

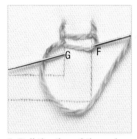

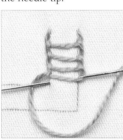

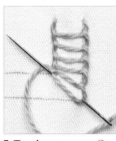

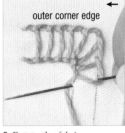

5 Pull the thread through. As the loop becomes smaller, insert the needle from F to G in the same manner as before.

6 Complete the stitch follow- ing step 4. Continue working stitches in the same manner for the required distance.

7 **Turning a corner.** On the inside corner, work the stitches very close together. The cross piece of a stitch will be diagonal at the corner.

8 Rotate the fabric on reaching outer edge of corner. Work the stitches very close together on the inside edge until the cross piece becomes horizontal again.

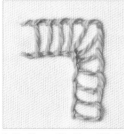

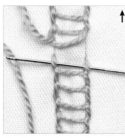

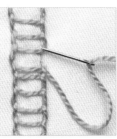

9 **Ending off a line.** Work two tiny straight stitches over the last loop, one on each marked line.

10 **To complete a border.** Work the second to last stitch. Pull through. Take the needle under the ends of the first stitch.

11 Pull the thread through. Take the needle to the back of the fabric inside the loop of the previous stitch.

12 Pull the thread through. **Completed open chain stitch.**

CHAIN STITCH – ROSETTE

This variation of twisted chain stitch produces a pretty, braided line. It is a useful outline stitch and equally effective in straight lines or curves. It can also be used in small circles to make floral motifs.

1 Bring the thread to the front at A on the right hand side of the upper line. Insert the needle into the fabric from B to C.

2 Wrap the thread under the tip of the needle in an anti-clockwise direction.

3 Continue wrapping until the thread crosses over itself. Pull the loop taut and hold in place with your left thumb (thumb not shown).

4 Keeping your thumb over the loop, pull the thread through in a downwards motion (thumb not shown).

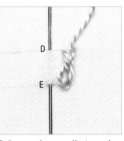

5 Slide the needle from right to left under the right hand section of thread. Do not go through the fabric.

6 Begin to pull the thread through.

7 Pull the thread through. **Completed first stitch.**

8 Insert the needle into the fabric from D to E.

9 Loop the thread in an anti-clockwise direction around the needle as before. Pull the thread through in a downward motion.

10 Slide the needle from right to left under the section of thread between the stitches. Do not go through the fabric.

11 Pull the thread through to complete the second stitch.

12 Continue working stitches in the same manner keeping them close together. **Completed line of rosette chain stitches.**

CHAIN STITCH – ROSE

Chain stitch roses may be stitched in either silk ribbon or thread. To work the chain stitches downwards, turn the fabric as you go. We used three shades of 4mm (³⁄₁₆") silk ribbon and a no.26 tapestry needle for our rose.

indicates top of fabric ↑

1 **Centre.** Using the darkest shade of ribbon, work a 2 wrap French knot for the centre.

2 **Inner petals.** Change to a lighter shade of ribbon. Bring it to the front at A, approximately 2mm (¹⁄₁₆") away from the French knot.

3 Insert the needle at A and re-emerge at B. Keeping the ribbon flat, loop it under the needle tip.

4 Pull through until the loop gently wraps around the ribbon. Do not pull too tightly as the stitch will become thin.

5 Rotate the fabric. Take the needle from B to C. Loop the ribbon under the needle tip.

6 Gently pull ribbon through. The second stitch anchors the first stitch.

7 Rotate the fabric. Insert the needle at C and re-emerge very close to A.

8 Loop the ribbon under the tip of the needle and gently pull through.

9 Take the needle to the back just over the loop.

10 Pull the ribbon through, forming a tiny straight stitch to anchor the last chain stitch. **Completed inner petals.**

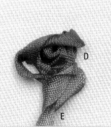

11 **Outer petals.** Using lightest shade, bring needle to front, just outside the first round (D). Work a chain stitch from D to E keeping the tension loose.

12 Following the diagram, work four more chain stitches. Anchor last chain stitch at D with a short straight stitch over the loop. **Completed chain stitch rose.**

CHINESE KNOT

Chinese knot is also known as blind knot, forbidden knot or Peking knot.

Chinese knots were used extensively in old Chinese embroideries.

Often they were the only stitches used and, when colour shading was a feature, the effect was truly sumptuous. The Chinese love of silk gave this work an even greater richness and lustre. Chinese knot may be used alone or as a filling stitch. The texture can be varied by leaving loops on the surface of the fabric.

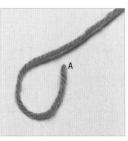

1 Secure the thread on the back. Bring it to the front at A. Loop the thread to the left.

2 Hold the loop onto the fabric with the left thumb and forefinger. The thread is trailed above.

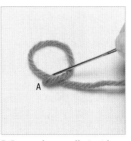

3 Pick up the loop with the left thumb and forefinger. Fold the loop over so the working thread crosses behind the emerging thread.

4 Lay the loop on the fabric.

5 Insert the needle inside the loop as close as possible to A (but not in the same hole).

6 Begin to tighten the loop onto the needle by pulling the working thread.

7 Tighten the loop around the needle and begin to push the needle through to the back. Keep the thread tension taut.

8 Pull the needle through to the back. Place your thumb over the loop and continue to pull the thread through to the back (thumb not shown).

9 Pull the thread all the way through until the knot sits snug-ly on the surface of the fabric. **Completed Chinese knot.**

10 **Chinese knot with a loop.** Work steps 1-5. Hold loop on fabric at required length with thumb. Pull the thread through (steps 6-9). Loop sits above knot.

COLONIAL KNOT

Also known as candlewicking knot. The colonial knot is similar in appearance, but slightly larger and higher than the more formal French knot.

Colonial knots can be worked alone or to fill a shape. They are more commonly stitched close together to form the lines within a candlewicking design.

1 Secure the thread on the back. Bring it to the front at the desired position for the knot.

2 Hold the thread loosely to the left. With the right hand, take the needle tip over the thread.

3 Hook the needle under the thread where it emerges from the fabric.

4 With your left hand, take the thread over the tip of the needle. Shorten the loop around the needle.

5 Take the thread under the tip of the needle. The thread now forms a figure eight around the needle.

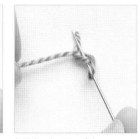

6 Take the tip of the needle to the back, approximately one or two fabric threads away from where it emerged.

7 Pull the wraps firmly against the fabric and begin to take the needle to the back.

8 Keeping the working thread taut, continue to push the needle through the knot to the back of the fabric.

9 Holding the knot and loop on the fabric with your thumb, continue to pull the thread through (thumb not shown).

10 Completed colonial knot.

COMBINATION STITCH – APPLE BLOSSOM FLOWER

Basic stitches may be combined to form pretty floral motifs. This blossom is a combination of fly stitch, straight stitch and French knots using two strands of 2 ply crewel wool, silk thread and a no.22 chenille needle.

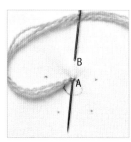

1 Petals. Draw a circle for the blossom centre. Mark five dots for the tips of the petals. Bring the needle to the front at A. Take a stitch from B to A.

2 Gently pull the thread through to form a straight stitch. The inner point of each petal will be on the circle.

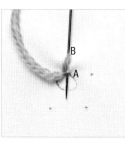

3 With the thread to the left of the needle, take a second stitch from B to A.

4 Pull needle through. Leaving thread loose, place needle under thread as stitch is positioned. This helps to create even stitches and 'plump' petals.

5 Keeping the needle under the stitch, pull the thread through until the second stitch lies to the left (and snug against) the first stitch.

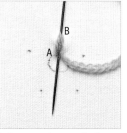

6 Remove the needle from under the stitches. With the thread to the right, take a third stitch from B to A.

7 Pull needle through. Leaving thread loose, re-position needle under stitches. Pull the thread through until the stitch lies to the right (snug against) first stitch.

8 Work 3-5 more stitches in the same way. Lay the last three stitches over the top of the petal. **Completed first petal.**

9 Work four more petals in the same manner, following steps 1-8. The petals just touch each other on the centre circle.

10 Straight stitches between petals. Change to yellow yarn. Work a straight stitch between each petal, stitching from the centre to where petals separate.

11 Petal tips. Change to light pink yarn. Work a straight stitch from centre of petal to tip. Work a fly stitch to hug each petal. Anchor the fly stitch at the tip.

12 Using silk, work 3 straight stitches over petals for high-lights. Work French knots using blended yellow and brown yarn for centre. **Completed blossom.**

COMBINATION STITCH – BUD

A combination of couching, whipping and straight stitch are used to create this lovely bud. The stem uses two strands of green 2 ply crewel wool and the petals use three shades of pink wool. The bud highlights are worked with silk thread.

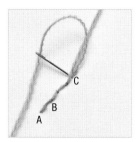

1 STEM Couching. Bring yarn to the front at A and lay along marked line. Bring new thread up at B. Couch laid thread to C. Leave the threads hanging.

2 Whipping. Using silk thread, bring to front at D. Slide needle under couched thread above B. Continue whipping to end of stem (C). Leave threads hanging.

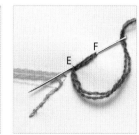

3 BUD Inner petal. Using darkest pink yarn, bring to front at E. Take a stitch from F to E and reposition the needle from F to E (see steps 1-3 on p.42).

4 To complete inner petal, work 4-5 more stitches between F and E, alternating from left to right. Place needle under stitches each time to keep them even.

5 Outer petals. Change thread. Bring to front, just left of the base of inner petal. Take needle to back on right side of petal, (approx two thirds up the side).

6 Pull the needle through. Work 2-3 more stitches using the same holes in the fabric. **Completed first outer petal.**

7 Change thread. Bring to front just to right of E. Take to back on left side of inner petal, about two thirds up the side. Work 2-3 more stitches using same holes.

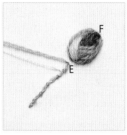

8 Sepals. Re-thread needle with laid yarn. Take to back at E, re-emerge at F. Work 2 straight stitches on each side of petals.

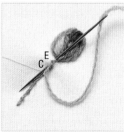

9 Work 3 straight stitches over the top of the petals to complete the sepals. **Calyx.** Re-thread the couching yarn, take the needle to back at E and re-emerge at C.

10 Pull the needle through. Work 4-5 more stitches using the same holes (as for the inner petal). End off the thread. **Completed calyx.**

11 Highlights. Using whipping thread, take needle to back of work at C and out at E. Work 3 straight stitches over calyx. Work 8-10 straight stitches over petals.

12 Stamens. Bring needle to front near F at top of bud. Turn work upside down. Work 2 fly stitches, 1 long and 1 short, each with long anchoring stitches.

CONCERTINA ROSE

Double-sided satin ribbon produces the best results for creating a concertina rose. We used single-sided ribbon and contrasting thread for photographic purposes only. Prepare a needle threaded with matching sewing thread.

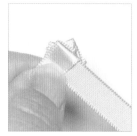

1 Cut a 25cm (10") length of ribbon. At the centre, make a right angled fold. Hold the fold in place with thumb and forefinger.

2 Fold the lower half of the ribbon over, keeping it at right angles to the upper half. The fold is on the edge of the ribbon. Hold in place.

3 Fold the lower half over the upper half again, ensuring the fold sits at the edge of the ribbon. Hold in place.

4 Repeat steps 2–3 seven times (ie fold the ribbon over fourteen more times). There will be a total of 16 folds.

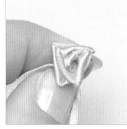
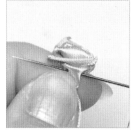

5 Hold the two ends of ribbon firmly in one hand and release the folds.

6 Still holding the ends in one hand, begin to pull one end with the other hand.

7 Continue pulling the same end until the rose forms and the folds sit close to your fingers.

8 Hold the two ends together. Take the pre-threaded needle through ribbon close to rose base. Pull thread through. Take needle up through rose centre.

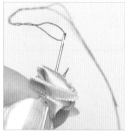
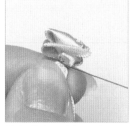

9 Pull the thread through. Take a tiny stitch as invisibly as possible and take the needle back through the centre to the base.

10 Pull thread through. Firmly wrap the thread around the base approximately three times.

11 Take thread through base of rose. Secure with a tiny back stitch. Trim ribbon only close to the base leaving a small stump. Press flat with thumb.

12 Use the same needle and thread to stitch the rose to the fabric. Take the stitches through both the stump and the base. **Completed concertina rose.**

CORAL STITCH

Coral stitch is one of the knotted stitches often used for crewel embroidery. It forms a beaded line of laid thread.

Contrasting texture can be obtained by working several rows close together to fill a shape. Aligning the knots in each row or dove-tailing the knots of one row into those of the previous rows, also produces an interesting effect.

Coral stitch is worked from right to left or down a line towards you.

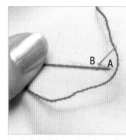

1 Draw a line on the fabric. Bring the thread to the front at the beginning of the line (A). Lay thread along line. Hold it along the line with the thumb.

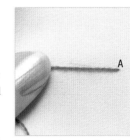

2 Still holding the thread, take the needle to the back at B just above the line (approx 3mm (⅛") to the left of A). A loop forms below the line.

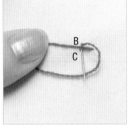

3 Still holding the thread, bring the needle to the front at C (just below B). The thread is under the tip of the needle.

4 Pull the thread through gently to form the first knot.

5 **First completed coral stitch.**

6 Lay the thread along the line. Take the needle to the back at D above the line (approx 3mm (⅛") left of knot). A loop forms below the line.

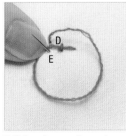

7 Bring the needle to the front at E below the laid thread (just below D).

8 Pull the thread through gently to form the second knot.

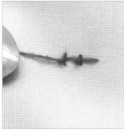

9 **Second completed coral stitch.**

10 Continue working stitches following steps 1-4. Finish with either a knot or a section of laid thread. Take the thread to the back and end off.

COUCHING

Couching is used to work outlines or to fill shapes. A thread or group of threads, is secured to the fabric with tiny evenly spaced stitches, worked with a second thread. Mark a line on the fabric.

  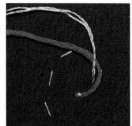 

1 Bring foundation thread to the front at the beginning of the line (A). Lay it along the line. Bring the second thread to the front just above laid thread.

2 Take the second thread to the back over the laid thread.

3 Pull the thread through, form-ing a very short straight stitch. Re-emerge a short distance along the laid thread.

4 Couch laid thread along line in same manner. When nearing end, take laid thread to back. Complete the couching stitches. End off both threads on back.

COUCHING – BOW

This stylised bow is fashioned from 45cm (17¾") of 2mm wide (¹⁄₁₆") pure silk ribbon. Tie the bow first. Secure it in place on the fabric using French knots and two strands of rayon thread. This delicate design is suitable for applying to lace.

1 Tie the ribbon into a bow with ties approx 9cm (3½") long. Draw a bow design onto the fabric. Position the bow onto the traced outline.

2 Place a pin across the bow knot. Catch the fabric on either side of the ribbon, taking care not to pierce the ribbon itself.

   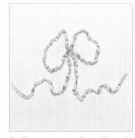

3 Bow. Folding ribbon, place the bow loops to follow the design lines. Pin near each fold, picking up fabric on either side, but not piercing the ribbon.

4 Ties. Fold at irregular inter-vals, 5-20mm (¼-¾") apart. Pin as you fold (as before) until entire bow is anchored to the fabric. Trim excess ribbon.

5 Work 3 wrap French knots at 4-8mm (³⁄₁₆-⁵⁄₁₆") intervals along the centre of the ribbon. Ensure a knot is positioned near the bow knot and at each fold.

6 Continue working French knots until the entire bow is secured to the fabric. **Completed couched bow.**

COUCHING – BOKHARA

In Bokhara couching, one continuous thread is used for both the laid thread and the anchoring stitches.

Bokhara couching is similar to Roumanian couching but in Bokhara couching, the diagonal anchoring stitch is short on the surface and long on the wrong side of the fabric. In Roumanian couching the reverse is the case. The distance between the diagonal stitches will vary according to the thread used.

Always work with the fabric in a hoop to prevent puckering. Draw the required shape onto the fabric.

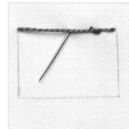

1 First laid stitch. Bring the thread to the front on the left hand side of the shape.

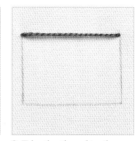

2 Take the thread to the back on the right hand side, forming a long straight stitch. Pull through until the thread lies loosely on the fabric.

3 First couching stitch. Bring the needle to the front, just under the straight stitch, a short distance from right hand edge.

4 Pull the thread through. Take it to the back just above the straight stitch and a little to the left of where it emerged.

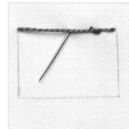

5 Pull through forming a short diagonal stitch over the straight stitch. Bring needle to front just under the straight stitch and a little further towards the left.

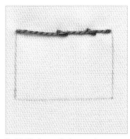

6 Pull thread through. Take it to the back in the same manner as before to form a second short diagonal stitch.

7 Continue working short diagonal stitches in the same way to the other end of the straight stitch. **Completed first row.**

8 Bring the needle to the front on left hand side just below first laid stitch. Work a second long straight stitch across the shape.

9 Bring thread to front just below second laid stitch (same distance from edge as before). Take to back between the two long stitches.

10 Continue working diagonal stitches along second stitch (the same intervals as the first laid stitch). Continue working rows of couching until shape is filled.

COUCHING – LATTICE

The foundation of this combination stitch is made from a grid of long diagonal stitches which are couched at the intersections with small cross stitches. Draw the shape onto the fabric.

   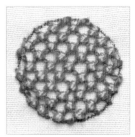

1 Work long diagonal straight stitches in one direction across the entire area. Space stitches approx 5mm (¼") apart. Work a second set in opposite direction.

2 **Couching.** Change thread. Bring it to the front just below the first intersection of two straight stitches on the lower left hand side. Take thread to back just above intersection.

3 Re-emerge just to the left of the intersection. Take the thread to the back on the right hand side of the intersection, forming a small cross.

4 Re-emerge just below the second intersection. Continue working crosses in the same manner, along the laid stitches, until all the intersections are couched in place.

Hints on using threads

Stranded threads

1 All stranded threads have a twist and working with the twist will help the thread remain smooth and glossy. With the thread between your thumb and forefinger, run your fingers up and down the thread. One way will feel slightly smoother than the other. The smooth way is with the twist. Thread the end you pull from the skein into the needle.

2 When using multiple strands, always separate them, then put them back together. 'Stripping' the thread gives a better stitch coverage.

3 Use lengths of thread no longer than 50cm (20"). Long threads eventually become tired and worn as the fabric abrades them.

4 If the thread untwists or overtwists, let the needle dangle freely. The thread will spin back to the correct amount of twist.

Metallic threads

1 Metallic thread can be difficult to work with and wears easily. Use short lengths to make it more manageable and to retain the lustre.

2 The section of thread in the eye of the needle wears quickly. Adjust the thread frequently or tie the tail of thread to the eye of the needle.

Rayon threads

1 Rayon threads have a mind of their own and can be difficult to use. Dampening the thread can make it more manageable. Moisten your fingertips and slowly pull the thread between them. This method ensures the thread does not become too damp.

2 Always strip the thread and then recombine the number of strands you wish to use.

3 Iron the thread to eliminate kinks. Place it on the ironing board and cover with a clean cloth. Pull the thread through while pressing firmly with a warm iron.

4 Use short lengths of thread to minimise twisting and tangling.

5 Place the thread in the freezer for a few hours. This reduces static electricity.

Variegated threads

1 Undo the skein of thread and lay it out so you can clearly see the range of colours. Lay sections of the same colour side by side. To obtain exactly the colours you want to use, cut selected sections from the thread.

2 Create your own 'variegated' thread by blending strands from different skeins and threading them into your needle together.

COUCHING – ROUMANIAN

Also known as Oriental laid stitch, figure stitch and antique couching. Roumanian couching is worked with a continuous thread. It is effective for covering large areas where a smooth, flat surface is desired. Use a hoop to keep the work taut.

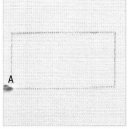

1 Mark the shape to be filled onto the fabric. Bring the thread to the front at A on the left side of the shape.

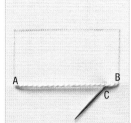

2 Take the needle to the back at B on the other side of the shape.

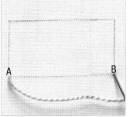

3 Pull the thread through. **Completed laid stitch.** Bring needle to the front at C directly under the laid stitch.

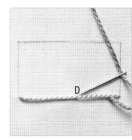

4 Take the needle over the laid stitch and to the back at D forming a diagonal stitch.

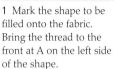

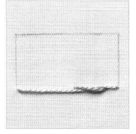

5 Pull the thread through until it sits loosely over the laid stitch. **First completed couching stitch.**

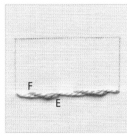

6 Work a second diagonal couching stitch from E to F in the same manner.

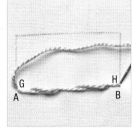

7 Bring the thread to the front at G, just above A on the marked line. Take the needle to the back at H just above B.

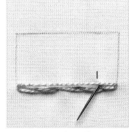

8 Pull through to form a second laid stitch. Bring needle to front at I, angling needle to emerge between the two laid stitches.

9 Take the needle over the second laid stitch and to the back at J, forming a diagonal stitch. Make a second diagonal stitch from K to L.

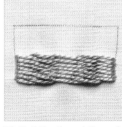

10 Pull the thread through. Keep an even tension and the stitches loose so they do not distort the fabric. Continue to work in the same manner.

11 Roumanian couching is usually worked using one thread colour. We used contrasting threads for photographic purposes only.

12 The petals of this variegated flower are embroidered with Roumanian couching.

COUCHING – TRELLIS

Also known as Jacobean couching. Trellis couching has a foundation of long straight stitches which are couched down with small cross stitches. As with most variations of couching, using a hoop prevents the foundation stitches from becoming distorted.

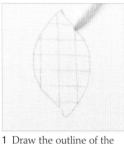

1 Draw the outline of the shape and mark the grid lines. Bring the thread to the front where one grid line meets the outline of the shape.

2 Take the thread to the back at the opposite side of the shape where the grid line meets the outline.

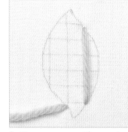

3 Re-emerge on the next line over. Pull the thread through.

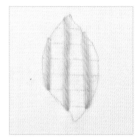

4 Take the thread to the back at the end of the grid line. Con- tinue until long straight stitches cover all marked grid lines.

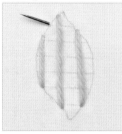

5 Bring the needle to the front on the outline, where it meets one grid line, at right angles to those already worked.

6 Take the needle over the previous straight stitches and to the back at the opposite end of the grid line.

7 Continue working long straight stitches across the shape until all the grid lines are covered. **Completed foundation.**

8 **Couching.** Change thread colour. Bring thread to front at lower left of intersection of first two straight stitches on the left side of the shape. Pull through.

9 Form a diagonal stitch by taking the thread to the back over the foundation stitches. Pull thread through. Re-emerge at lower left of intersection of next two straight stitches.

10 Continue working stitches to the end of the row. Bring the thread to the front on the lower right of the intersection.

11 Form a cross by taking the thread to the back over the previous diagonal stitch. Re-emerge at lower right of the next intersection to the left.

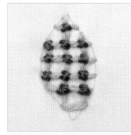

12 Work all other rows following steps 8-11. **Completed trellis couching.**

CRETAN STITCH

Cretan stitch is a filling stitch with a plaited centre, particularly useful for leaf shapes. A variety of effects can be achieved by altering the distance between stitches, the amount of fabric picked up and the angle of the needle.

 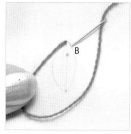  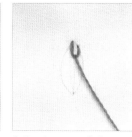

1 Mark the shape of a leaf with two curved lines inside the leaf shape. Bring the needle to the front at A. Hold the thread under the thumb.

2 Take the needle to the back at B. The thread forms a loop below the needle.

3 Pull the thread through the fabric leaving a small loop. Bring the needle to the front at C on the right inner curved line below B.

4 Continue to pull the thread through until the loop sits snug-ly below the emerging thread. **Completed first stitch.**

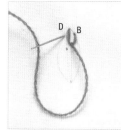   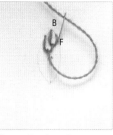

5 Loop the thread as shown and hold under thumb (thumb not shown). Take the needle to the back at D (opposite B) near the top on the left outside line.

6 Pull the thread through leaving a loop. Bring the needle to the front at E (inside loop) on the left inner curved line.

7 Pull the thread through until the loop sits snugly below the emerging thread. **Completed second stitch.**

8 Loop the thread as shown and hold under thumb (thumb not shown). Take the needle to the back at F on the right outside line below B.

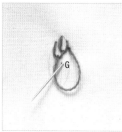   

9 Pull thread through leaving a small loop. Bring the needle to the front at G (inside loop) on the right inner curved line.

10 Continue to pull the thread through until the loop sits snugly below the emerging thread. **Completed third stitch.**

11 Follow steps 5-7 to work the fourth stitch from H to I.

12 Continue working stitches, alternating along inner curved lines. To anchor the last stitch take needle to back just below last loop.

CROSS STITCH

Cross stitch is probably the oldest and best known of all embroidery stitches. It is usually worked on even-weave fabric, using a tapestry needle. Once the work has begun, ensure the top half stitches lie in the same direction. Using guidelines or counting fabric threads, ensures even-sized stitches.

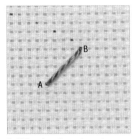

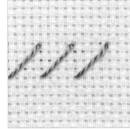

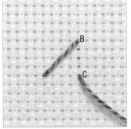

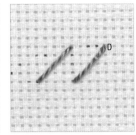

1 **First row of half stitches.** Secure the thread on the back or begin with a waste knot. Bring the thread to the front at A. Pull the thread through.

2 Take the thread to the back at B, above and to the right of A. Pull the thread through to form a diagonal stitch.

3 Re-emerge at C, directly below B. Pull the thread through.

4 Take the needle to the back at D, forming a second stitch parallel to the first stitch. Pull the thread through.

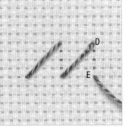

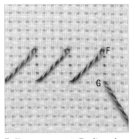

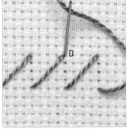

5 Re-emerge at E, directly below D. Pull the thread through.

6 Continue in the same manner until the required number of half stitches are worked.

7 Re-emerge at G, directly below the end of the last stitch (F). Pull the thread through. **Completed first row of half stitches.**

8 **Second row of half stitches.** Using the same hole in the fabric, take the needle to the back at D.

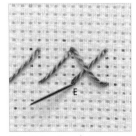

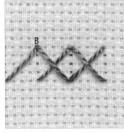

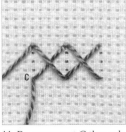

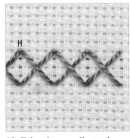

9 Pull the thread through to form the first cross stitch. Re-emerge at E through the same hole in the fabric.

10 Pull the thread through. Take the needle to the back at B using the same hole in the fabric. Pull the thread through.

11 Re-emerge at C through the same hole in the fabric. Pull the thread through.

12 Take the needle to the back at H and pull the thread through. Complete row in same manner. **Completed cross stitches.**

CROSS STITCH – LONG-ARMED

This stitch is known by several different names – long-legged cross stitch, plaited Slav stitch, Portuguese stitch and twist stitch.

It is worked from left to right, usually on canvas but also on even-weave fabrics. Like cross stitch, once the work has begun, all the top half stitches should lie in the same direction.

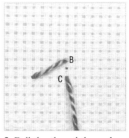

1 Bring the thread to the front at A. Take the needle to the back at B.

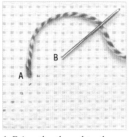

2 Pull the thread through to form a long diagonal straight stitch. Re-emerge at C, directly below B. Pull the thread through.

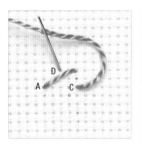

3 Take the needle to the back at D, approximately half the distance between A and C.

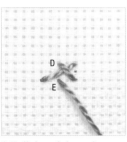

4 Pull thread through to com-plete the first stitch. Bring the needle to the front at E, directly below D. Pull thread through.

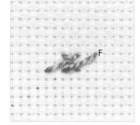

5 Take the needle to the back at F. Pull the thread through forming a second long diagonal straight stitch.

6 Continue working stitches in the same manner. **Completed long-armed cross stitch.**

CROSS AND STRAIGHT STITCH COMBINATION

Here we show cross and straight stitch combination worked with each stitch being completed individually. This stitch can also be worked in separate steps across a row. Ensure the top stitches all lie in the same direction.

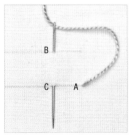

1 Bring the thread to the front at A. Take the needle to the back at B, diagonally opposite A. Re-emerge at C, below B and to the left of A.

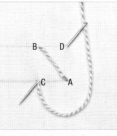

2 Pull the thread through. Take the needle to the back at D, directly above A. Re-emerge at C to begin the straight stitch.

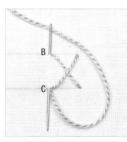

3 Pull the thread through. Take the needle from B to C using the same holes in the fabric.

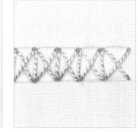

4 Pull thread through. Continue working stitches following steps 1–3. **Completed cross stitches with straight stitches in between.**

CROW'S FOOT

A crow's foot is a tailoring technique, similar to an arrowhead, which is used to strengthen the stress points on a garment. Here it is worked as a surface stitch to produce a small decorative triangular motif on plain-weave fabric.

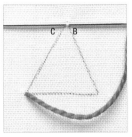

1 Draw a triangle on the fabric. Bring the thread to the front at A on the lower left hand corner.

2 Insert the needle at B and re-emerge at C, picking up one fabric thread.

3 Pull the thread through.

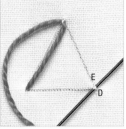

4 Take the needle to the back at D on the lower right hand corner and re-emerge at E picking up one fabric thread.

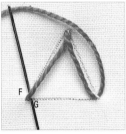

5 Pull the thread through. Take the needle from F to G through the fabric.

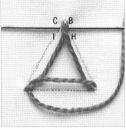

6 Pull the thread through. Take the needle from H to I (just below B and C), picking up a slightly larger piece of fabric.

7 Pull the thread through. Take the needle from J to K (just next to D and E), picking up slightly more of the fabric as before.

8 Pull the thread through. Take the needle from L to M, picking up slightly more of the fabric.

9 Continue working stitches in a clockwise direction, picking up slightly larger pieces of fabric in each round.

10 **Completed crow's foot.**

CUTWORK EMBROIDERY

Cutwork is a form of openwork embroidery which includes blanket-stitched bars and eyelet holes. The embroidery is completed before cutting away any fabric. We used coton á broder and a no.9 'sharp' needle.

1 Mark design on fabric. Work a running stitch outline around all areas to be blanket-stitched. When reaching first bar, take needle to inside of shape and take a small stitch.

2 Pull the thread through. Take a long stitch back to the beginning of the bar, then across to the inside of the shape again in the same manner.

3 Blanket stitch over these three strands until they are completely covered and the thread is back at the start. The stitches do not pierce the fabric. Do not stretch the bar.

4 Continue working running stitch and the blanket-stitched bars until the outer section is complete. Work running stitch around the inner section.

5 Starting on the outside of the design, work close blanket stitch around the areas to be cut. The ridge of the blanket stitch lies against the area to be cut away.

6 Work blanket stitch along the inner line of the design covering the opposite ends of the bars. You may wish to turn your work as you stitch.

7 **Completed blanket stitching.**

8 **Cutting the fabric.** Using the point of a pair of very sharp, fine embroidery scissors, pierce the fabric in the centre of one area to be cut away. With the right side up, clip towards the blanket stitch edge.

9 Cut away the fabric as close to the blanket stitching as possible. Angle the scissors under the ridged edge and take great care not to cut any of the edging stitches or bars. **Completed cutwork heart.**

DANISH KNOT

This easy knot can be worked singly as an accent stitch or close together to create textured clusters. It is a delightful pebbly knot adding quite heavy texture when worked en masse in thick, shiny thread such as perle no.3 cotton.

The substantial nature of this knot gives subtle contrasts between light and shade when different weights and colours of thread are used.

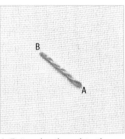

1 Bring the thread to the front at A and take a short diagonal straight stitch to B. This is the foundation stitch.

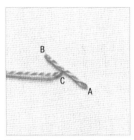

2 Bring the needle to the front at C at the left of the foundation stitch, halfway between A and B. Pull thread through.

3 With the thread below the needle, slide the needle under the foundation stitch above C. Take care not to catch the thread or the fabric.

4 Pull the thread gently.

5 Continue pulling the thread through until the knot lies gently around the foundation stitch.

6 With the thread below the needle, slide the needle under the foundation stitch(just above A). The needle is at right angles to the foundation stitch.

7 Begin to pull the thread through gently.

8 Continue pulling the thread through until the second knot rests on the foundation stitch.

9 Take the needle to the back close to the knot and finish off.

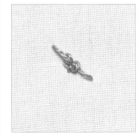

10 Completed Danish knot.

DETACHED CHAIN

Also known as lazy daisy stitch. Detached chain stitch is a looped stitch, which can be worked alone or in groups. It can also be used as a filling stitch with individual stitches placed at regular intervals over the space to be filled.

1 Bring the needle to the front at the base of the stitch (A). Take needle to the back as close as possible to A. Re-emerge at the tip of the stitch.

2 Loop the thread in an anti-clockwise direction under the tip of the needle.

3 Keeping your left thumb over the loop, pull the thread through (thumb not shown). The tighter you pull, the thinner the stitch will become.

4 To anchor the stitch, take the thread to the back just over the loop. **Completed detached chain.**

DETACHED CHAIN – FLOWERS

Detached chain stitch can be used to create a variety of flowers and leaves. Here we show two methods to stitch different daisies, with each petal being a single detached chain.

1 **Five petal daisy.** Bring the needle to the front at A (centre). Take it to back at A and re-emerge at B. Loop the thread under needle tip.

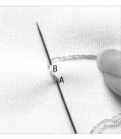

2 Pull thread through gently. Anchor the stitch by taking the needle to the back over the loop (just above B). **Completed first detached chain petal.**

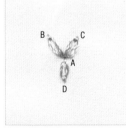

3 Pull the thread through and bring the needle up at A. Work two more stitches from A–C and A–D. The three petals form a 'Y' shape.

4 Work the fourth and fifth stitches midway between C & D and B & D. **Completed five petal daisy.**

5 **Eight petal daisy.** Mark a tiny circle for the flower centre. Work four petals from the centre circle in the form of a cross.

6 Work four more petals in the spaces between the previous four. You may wish to fill the centre with French knots. **Completed eight petal daisy.**

DETACHED CHAIN – FRENCH KNOT COMBINATION FLOWER

This combination of stitches is used to complete detached chain flowers. The French knots form the tips of the petals. Alternative names for detached chain are, daisy stitch, lazy daisy stitch, knotted knot stitch, loop stitch, picot stitch, tied loop stitch, tail chain stitch and link powdering stitch.

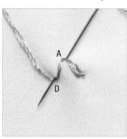

1 **Right petal.** Bring thread to front at A. Take the needle to the back at A and re-emerge at B. The needle is angled to the right. Loop thread under needle tip.

2 Wrap the thread twice in an anti-clockwise direction around the needle tip.

3 Holding knot under thumb (thumb not shown), pull thread gently towards you. Pull knot to the right. Take thread to back at C. This forms a small 'foot'.

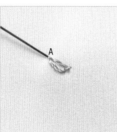

4 **Completed right petal.** The detached chain is now anchored with a French knot. To begin the left petal, bring the needle and thread to the front at A.

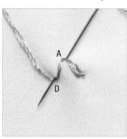

5 **Left petal.** Take the needle from A to D. The needle is angled to the left. Loop thread clockwise under the needle tip.

6 Wrap the thread around the needle twice in a clockwise direction.

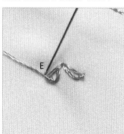

7 Repeat step 3 anchoring the chain to the left at E forming a small 'foot'.

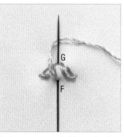

8 **Centre petal** (detached chain only). Bring the thread to the front at F. Take the needle to the back at F again and re-emerge at G. Loop thread under needle tip.

9 To anchor the petal take the needle to the back just over the loop at A and end off.

10 **Completed flower.**

DETACHED CHAIN – BLANKET STITCH COMBINATION

Using blanket stitches with detached chain gives a flower shape with a continuous edge, such as this daffodil trumpet.

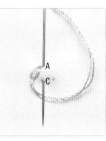

1 Bring thread to front at A. Loop thread as shown. Take the needle from A to B. The needle is angled to the left.

2 Pull thread through forming a detached chain. Take the needle from A to C. Loop the thread under the needle tip.

3 Pull thread through to form a blanket stitch. Work another to the right. To end off, take thread to back just over loop.

DETACHED WHEATEAR STITCH

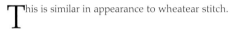

This is similar in appearance to wheatear stitch.

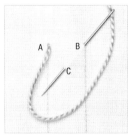

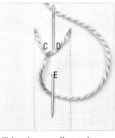

1 Mark two parallel lines down the fabric to keep stitches even. Bring thread to front at A. Take needle from B to C, halfway between lines.

2 Loop the thread under the tip of the needle.

3 Pull the thread through in a downward movement. Hold thread taut under your thumb.

4 Take the needle to the back at D, very close to C. Re-emerge at E, directly below. Loop the thread under the needle tip.

5 Pull the thread through in a downward movement until the loop rests snugly on the emerg-ing thread.

6 Take the needle to the back directly below E (just over the loop).

7 Pull the thread through. **Completed first detached wheatear stitch**.

8 Continue working stitches, positioning them close together or further apart as required.

DRIZZLE STITCH – FLOWER

Drizzle stitch is a Brazilian embroidery stitch, best worked with a straw needle. It is created from cast-ons like those used in cast-on stitch. The stitches are very effective when clustered together as shown below.

1 Draw a 6mm (¼") circle on the fabric. Knot the thread and bring it to the front on the edge of the circle.

2 Insert the needle halfway into the fabric just next to the thread. Unthread the needle.

3 With your finger facing you, place the thread over your left index finger.

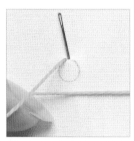

4 Rotate your finger towards you. Keep the thread taut and looped around your index finger.

5 Continue to rotate your finger until the thread is wrapped around the finger.

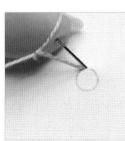

6 Keeping tension on the thread, place the tip of your finger on the end of the needle.

7 Slip the loop off your finger and onto the needle.

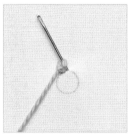

8 Pull the thread tight, slipping the loop down the needle onto fabric. This is the first cast-on.

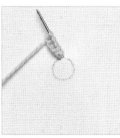

9 Work four more cast-ons in the same manner. Pull each one firmly and pack them down onto the needle.

10 Re-thread the needle. Pull the needle and thread through the cast-ons. **First completed drizzle stitch.**

11 Continue working stitches around the circle in the same manner.

12 Fill the centre of the circle with drizzle stitches. **Completed drizzle stitch flower.**

ERMINE FILLING STITCH

Ermine filling stitch is an easy stitch to work. If worked in black thread on white fabric, it looks very much like ermine tails, hence the name. Mark two parallel lines on the fabric to help keep the stitches even.

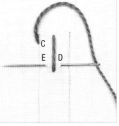

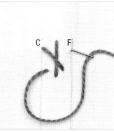

1 Bring the thread to the front at A. Take it to the back at B and re-emerge at C (slightly lower than A). Pull through to form the centre straight stitch.

2 Take the thread through the fabric from right to left (D to E), just above the end of the central straight stitch.

3 Pull the thread through. Take the needle to the back at F (directly opposite C).

4 Pull the thread through. **Completed ermine filling stitch.**

Hints on using hoops

Hoops are designed to hold the fabric taut while stitching, thus preventing unsightly puckering in your work.

Embroidery stitches fall into two categories – those that are 'sewn' (eg chain stitch, stem stitch, fly stitch and bullion knots) and those that are 'stabbed' (eg French knots, straight stitch, satin stitch, split stitch, running stitch and couching).

Sewn stitches are generally worked in one movement and from one side of the fabric only. These stitches are best worked without a hoop so the fabric can be manipulated.

Stabbed stitches are generally worked in two steps. The needle is taken to the back of the fabric and the thread pulled through before returning the needle to the front.

While some stitches can be either 'sewn' or 'stabbed' (eg satin stitch), stabbing produces a better result.

A hoop is a valuable aid when working stabbed stitches.

1 If possible, always use a good quality hoop. Hoops that can be tightened with a screwdriver are best as they can hold the fabric more firmly than other hoops.

2 Bind the inner ring of wooden hoops with cotton tape. This helps the hoop hold the fabric firmly and is gentler on the fabric.

3 Hold the hoop only with your fingers so you don't alter the tension of the fabric. Avoid touching the fabric in the hoop.

sewn

stabbed

EYELETS

These embroidered holes are the basis of traditional white-on-white Broderie Anglaise or Swiss embroideries. They are also used in Madeira and Venetian embroidery.

Eyelets have a small central hole, which is surrounded by running stitches and then covered by short, regular, overcasting stitches. The beauty of this technique is in the regularity of the stitches. Mark a tiny circle on the fabric.

1 With right side up, and using a dressmaker's awl, pierce the fabric on the marked circle. **Do this carefully**. The awl should gently separate the fabric fibres.

2 With right side of work facing, take a small running stitch just outside the hole. Pull the thread through, leaving a tail of approx 3mm (⅛").

3 Work small running stitches around the circle. On the last stitch, take the needle through the first stitch, splitting the stitch. Pull the thread through.

4 Re-pierce the hole with the awl. Bring the needle and thread to the front of the work just outside a running stitch.

5 Take the needle through the pierced hole and bring it to the right side directly alongside the emerging thread. Pull the thread through.

6 Holding the emerging thread under the thumb, take the needle through pierced hole and bring to the right side alongside pre-vious stitch (thumb not shown).

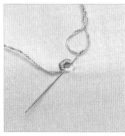

7 Closely overcast edge of eye-let as shown. Keep turning work to maintain consistent fanning of stitches. Keep an even tension on the closely worked stitches.

8 Finish overcasting and take the thread to the back through the hole.

9 To end off, take the thread under the overcast stitches on the back.

10 If necessary, use the awl to carefully re-punch the hole from the back. This helps to 'settle' the thread and fabric.

wrong side of fabric

EYELET FLOWERS

These tiny flowers consist of an eyelet centre and four padded satin stitch petals, all worked with one strand of silk thread. The eyelet overcasting stitches need to be worked very firmly. The petals require a looser tension.

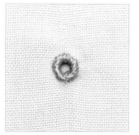

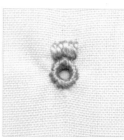

1 Work an eyelet as shown on the previous page.

2 **Petals.** To work the first petal, bring the needle to the front on the outer edge of the eyelet. Work 4 vertical satin stitches from left to right.

3 Working back over the first layer of stitches, work another 5-6 satin stitches. **Completed first petal.**

4 Work 3 more petals around the eyelet in the same manner. **Completed flower.**

SHAPED EYELET

Large eyelets can be worked in a variety of shapes. Leaves, petals, ovals, triangles or large circles are some of the shapes appearing in Broderie Anglaise or cutwork designs. These are stitched in a similar manner to the eyelets on page 62, however the fabric is cut rather than pierced with an awl or stilletto. Lengthen the overcasting stitches on the points and corners of the tear-drop and triangular eyelets.

Always work on a fabric with a fine, firm texture and use twisted threads such as stranded cotton and silk.

1 Draw the shape onto the fab-ric. Work running stitch just out-side the outline. For a teardrop or petal, cut fabric into segments within the outline as shown.

2 Cut larger circles and triangles into segments as shown.

3 Turn the fabric flaps to the back in the centre of the shape and finger press.

4 Overcast the eyelet, catching the flaps with the stitches. Clip away any excess fabric on the wrong side. **Completed eyelet.**

FAGGOTING

Faggoting, or twisted insertion stitch, can be used to join together two pieces of fabric. It produces an attractive join with an open, lacy look. Strong cotton or linen thread should be used. The measurements below are intended as a guide only.

1 On a piece of stiff paper, rule two parallel lines 3mm (⅛") apart. Rule vertical lines (cross-bars) between the parallel lines at 3mm (⅛") intervals.

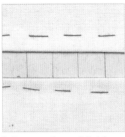

2 Press under and finish the seam allowance on each piece of the fabric. Align the folded edges with the parallel lines and tack the fabric to the paper.

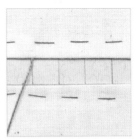

3 Knot the thread. Take the thread through the fold of the seam allowance in the upper piece of fabric, emerging at the top of a crossbar.

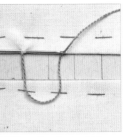

4 Take a tiny back stitch near the fold to secure the thread.

5 Pull thread through. Loop to right above needle tip. Keeping needle vertical, pick up a few threads on fold of lower fabric at the bottom of next crossbar.

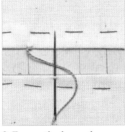

6 Ensure the loop of thread is behind the tip of the needle.

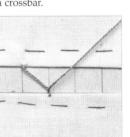

7 Pull the thread through.

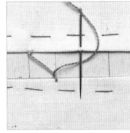

8 Loop the thread to the right. Pick up a few threads on the fold of the upper fabric at the tip of the next crossbar.

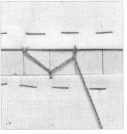

9 Ensure the loop is behind the needle. Pull the thread through.

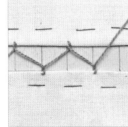

10 Continue in the same manner to the end.

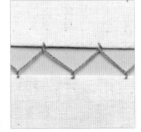

11 Remove tacking stitches and paper. To end off, work two tiny back stitches near a folded edge on wrong side. Press and spray starch the stitches to set them. **Completed faggoting.**

FEATHER STITCH

Feather stitch is usually worked on fine fabric with one or two strands of thread. It is a delicate stitch, often used to decorate baby and children's clothing. The stitch varies greatly in appearance, depending on the angle of the needle and the length of the stitches.

The tension, needle angle and stitch length must be kept consistent throughout to ensure even stitches.

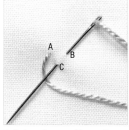

1 Bring the needle to the front at A. Loop the thread to the right and take the needle from B to C. The loop is under the needle.

2 Pull the thread through in a downward movement, holding the thread firmly with the thumb. **Completed first stitch.**

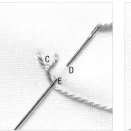

3 Take needle from D to E. Loop thread under needle tip.

4 Pull thread through. **Completed second stitch.**

5 Loop thread under needle and hold. Take needle from F to G.

6 Continue, following steps 3-5. Finish with a tiny stitch over loop.

FEATHER STITCH – CLOSED

This stitch is worked downwards between two parallel lines.

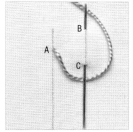

1 Rule lines on fabric. Bring thread to front at A on left line. Pull thread through. Take needle from B to C on right line. Loop thread under the needle tip.

2 Pull the thread through in a downward motion until the loop rests snugly on the emerging thread.

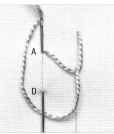

3 Take the needle from A to D, using the same hole in the fabric at A. Ensure the thread is looped under the tip of the needle.

4 Pull the thread through as before. Continue working stitches from side to side in the same manner. **Completed closed feather stitch.**

FEATHER STITCH – DOUBLE AND TRIPLE

The double and triple styles of feather stitch are attractive variations of basic feather stitch. Usually worked in a regular pattern these variations produce a delightful lacy effect.

To keep the stitches even, rule three parallel lines on the fabric for double feather stitch and four lines for triple feather stitch.

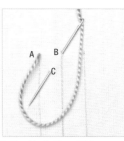

1 Double feather stitch. Emerge at A. Insert needle at B, directly opposite A. Re-emerge at C, halfway between and slightly lower than A and B.

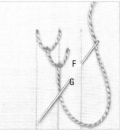

2 Loop the thread to the right and under the needle.

3 Pull the thread through in a downward movement. Hold the thread firmly with your thumb. **Completed first stitch.**

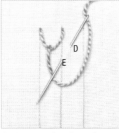

4 Keeping the thread taut, loop it to the right. Take the needle from D to E. Ensure the loop is under the tip of the needle.

5 Pull the thread through in a downward movement and hold it firmly with your thumb (thumb not shown).

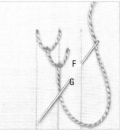

6 Keeping the thread taut, loop it to the right. Take the needle from F to G. Ensure the loop is under the tip of the needle.

7 Pull the thread through as before.

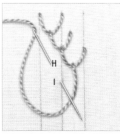

8 Loop the thread to the left and hold in place firmly with your thumb. Take needle from H to I, ensuring the loop is under the tip of the needle.

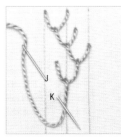

9 Pull the thread through as before. Again, loop the thread to the left and hold in place firmly with your thumb. Take the needle from J to K.

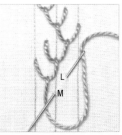

10 Pull the thread through as before. Loop the thread to the right and hold in place firmly with your thumb. Take the nee-dle from L to M.

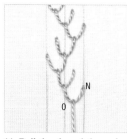

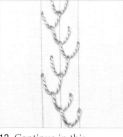

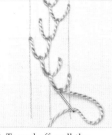

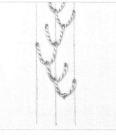

11 Pull the thread through as before. Again, loop the thread to the right. Holding the thread firmly, take a stitch from N to O and pull through.

12 Continue in this manner, working the sequence of two stitches to the left and two stitches to the right each time.

13 To end off, pull the thread through for the last stitch. Take the needle to the back over the looped thread, just below where it emerged.

14 Pull the thread through and secure on the back. **Completed double feather stitch.**

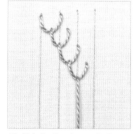

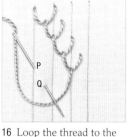

15 Triple feather stitch variation. Work steps 1-7 and then work one more stitch.

16 Loop the thread to the left and hold firmly. Take the needle to the back at P, on the left hand side directly opposite the last stitch. Re-emerge at Q.

17 Ensure the thread is under the tip of the needle and pull through as before. Work three stitches with the thread looped to the right.

18 Work the next stitch follow-ing step 16. Continue in this sequence to the end of the row. **Completed triple feather stitch variation.**

FEATHER STITCH – SINGLE

In single feather stitch, the 'arms' of the stitch lie to one side. Single feather stitch is often used in smocking and looks quite similar to blanket stitch.

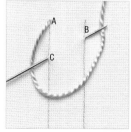

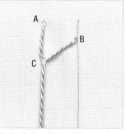

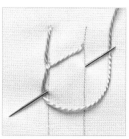

1 Bring the thread to front at A and pull through. Loop thread to the right. Take the needle from B to C. Ensure the thread is under the tip of the needle.

2 Pull the thread through in a downward movement.

3 Make a second stitch in the same manner.

4 Continue stitching, making sure the spaces between the stitches are even. **Completed single feather stitch.**

FEATHER STITCH – SPANISH KNOTTED

This is a decorative stitch with a braided appearance, particularly useful for borders.

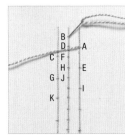

1 Mark 3 parallel lines. Bring the thread to front at A on the right hand line. Hold the thread to the left. Insert needle at B.

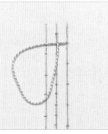

2 Loop the thread in an anti-clockwise direction. Pull thread through gently to form a circle.

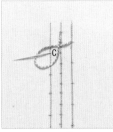

3 Continue pulling thread until a small loop remains. Bring the needle to the front at C inside the circle.

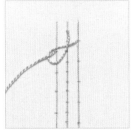

4 Pull through gently keeping the left thumb on the circle (thumb not shown).

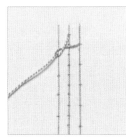

5 Pull the thread through until the thread rests against the emerging thread. **Completed first stitch.**

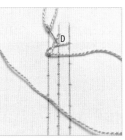

6 Loop the thread clockwise below the stitch. Insert needle at D level with A on centre line.

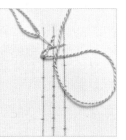

7 With the right thumb and forefinger, pick up the thread in front of the needle and form a whole circle of thread.

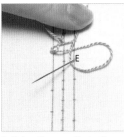

8 Bring the needle to the front at E inside the circle of thread.

9 Pull the thread gently through the circle to complete the second stitch.

10 **Completed second stitch.**

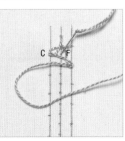

11 Holding thread to left, take needle to the back at F on the centre line level with C and below D.

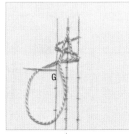

12 Pull the thread through leaving a small loop on the front. Emerge at G inside the circle of thread.

It is worked towards you, using three drawn parallel lines. The secrets of successfully completing this stitch are even tension, accurate spacing and lots of practice. Work slowly and carefully, especially when forming the loops. Spanish knotted feather stitch can be worked open or closed, depending on the effect required.

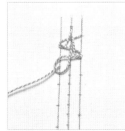

13 Begin to pull the thread through.

14 Pull the thread through, holding thread firmly. Arrange knot carefully with needle to keep it even and firmly on the fabric. **Completed third stitch.**

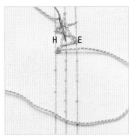

15 Form a loop clockwise under the stitch and insert the needle through to the back at H, below F on the centre line and level with E.

16 Re-emerge at I on the right hand line and inside the loop.

17 Pull the thread through.

18 Arrange the loop with the needle as before.

19 **Completed fourth stitch.**

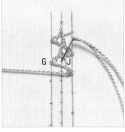

20 Form a loop to the left. Take the needle to the back at J on the centre line, level with G and below H.

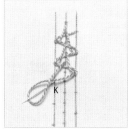

21 Bring the needle to the front at K inside the circle of thread.

22 Pull the thread through. Complete the fifth stitch and arrange the loop with the needle.

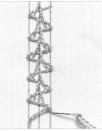

23 Continue in the same manner to the desired length. To finish take the needle to the back on the outside of a loop, forming a small couching stitch.

24 **Spanish knotted feather stitches worked closely together.**

FISHBONE STITCH

 ishbone stitch is a close fill-in stitch with a plaited centre suitable for working shapes such as borders, leaves, feathers or wings. When used for leaves the stitches cross at the centre and the plaited effect forms the central vein.

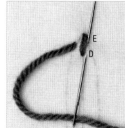

1 Straight fishbone stitch. Mark the outline of the shape and central line on the fabric. Bring the thread to the front at A on the centre line.

2 Take the needle from B, at the end of the line, to C. The thread is to the right of the needle.

3 Pull the thread through. With the thread to the left, take the needle from D to E.

4 Pull the thread through. This forms the first half of the first fishbone stitch.

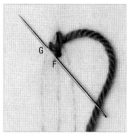

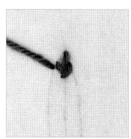

5 With the thread to the right, take the needle from F to G.

6 Pull the thread through. **Completed first fishbone stitch.**

7 With the thread to the left, take the needle from H to I.

8 Pull the thread through, and repeat steps 5 and 6. **Completed second fishbone stitch.**

9 Continue stitching alternating from left to right, forming a straight line of fishbone stitch. **Completed straight fishbone stitch.**

10 Curved fishbone stitch. Follow steps 1 to 8, until the shape begins to curve. On the curve, begin to increase the distance between the stitches on the outside edge.

11 Work down the shape, decreasing the distance between the stitches on the inside curve as well as increasing the distance on the outside curve.

12 Continue stitching. The sharper the curve, the greater the distance between the stitch-es on the outside line. **Completed curved fishbone stitch.**

FISHBONE STITCH – RAISED

Also known as overlapping herringbone stitch. This stitch is a simple variation of basic fishbone stitch. Here the stitches are taken right across the shape, rather than to a central line, to make a raised effect. Draw a shape on the fabric and mark the centre.

1 Bring the thread to the front at A at the top of the shape. Take the needle to the back at B (the central mark).

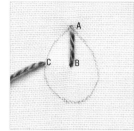

2 Pull the thread through. Bring the thread to the front at C, on the outline directly across from B. Pull the thread through.

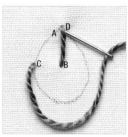

3 Take the thread to the back at D on the marked line, very close and to the right of A.

4 Pull the thread through. Emerge at E, on the marked line, very close and to the left of A. Pull thread through.

5 Take the needle to the back t F, on the outline directly oppo-site C.

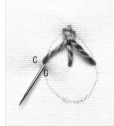

6 Pull the thread through and emerge at G, on the marked line just below C.

7 Pull the thread through. Take the thread to the back on the opposite side just below D.

8 Pull the thread through. Bring the needle to the front on the opposite side just below E.

9 Pull the thread through. Take the thread to the back on the opposite side just below F.

10 Pull the thread through and re-emerge on the opposite side just below G.

11 Continue working stitches in the same manner, ensuring they cross near the centre.

12 **Completed raised fish-bone stitch.**

FLY STITCH

Fly stitch is an open detached chain stitch with many possible variations. It is worked in the shape of a 'V' or 'Y' depending on the length of the anchoring stitch.

1 Bring the thread to the front at A. This will be the left hand side of the stitch.

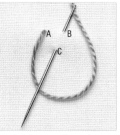

2 Take the needle to the back at B and re-emerge at C. Loop the thread under the tip of the needle and to the right.

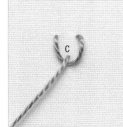

3 Hold the loop in place under the left thumb (thumb not shown). Pull the needle through until the looped thread lies snugly against C.

4 Take the thread to the back at the required distance below C to anchor the fly stitch. **Completed fly stitch.**

FLY STITCH – TWISTED

A variation of fly stitch, this stitch can be used to form the calyxes for buds.

The stalks can be varied in length to suit the design.

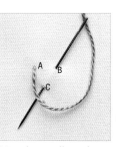

1 Bring the needle to the front at A. Take the needle to the back at B and re-emerge at C. The needle is under the thread.

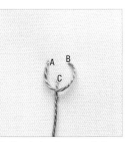

2 Gently begin to pull the needle through. The loop is over the thread.

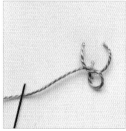

3 Take the needle over and through the loop. Begin to pull the thread through.

4 Pull thread through until the stitch lies flat on the fabric. To anchor the twisted fly stitch, take the needle to the back at D for the required length.

5 Pull the thread through. **Completed twisted fly stitch with long anchoring stitch.** In short-stalked twisted fly stitches, D is just below C.

6 Rose with double twisted fly stitch.

FLY STITCH – LEAF

Five to eight fly stitches are used to form each leaf. A smocker's knot is worked at the base to complete each one. The leaves can be made to curl either to the right or to the left. Begin by drawing a leaf shape with a centre vein onto the fabric.

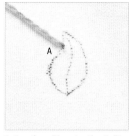

1 **Leaf curling to the left.** Bring the needle to the front at A on the left side of the leaf below the point. Pull the thread through.

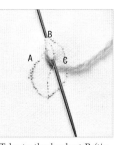

2 Take to the back at B (tip of leaf). Bring to the front at C on the centre vein. The thread is under the needle.

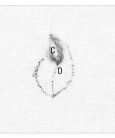

3 Pull the thread through. To anchor the fly stitch, take the needle to the back at D below C. **Completed first fly stitch.**

4 Work a second fly stitch just below the first, keeping the left side shorter than the right. This ensures the leaf curls to the left.

5 Work 3-6 more fly stitches down the leaf, to fill in the shape. The last stitch is anchored at the base of the leaf.

6 **Smocker's knot.** Bring the needle to front 2mm (1/16") away from base of leaf. Slide the needle under last anchoring stitch, to form the first loop.

7 Follow the instructions on page 118 following steps 3-10 to complete the knot. **Completed smocker's knot at the base of the leaf.**

8 **Highlights.** Using one strand of silk thread, bring needle up at outside of leaf. Take needle to back at centre vein, keeping stitch parallel to fly stitches.

9 Work approx 6-8 more straight stitches parallel to the fly stitches. The stitches vary in length and are randomly placed. **Completed leaf.**

10 **Completed left curling fly stitch leaves.**

11 For a leaf curling to the right, work the right side of each fly stitch shorter than the left side.

12 **Completed right curling fly stitch leaves.**

FOLDED RIBBON ROSE

These decorative roses can be made from different widths and types of ribbon. The size of the rose is determined by the width of the ribbon and the number of folds. Each rose is formed individually and then attached to the fabric. Prepare a needle threaded with matching sewing thread.

1 Centre. Hold length of ribbon horizontally in left hand. With right thumb and forefinger, fold right end over for approx 2cm (¾") at a 90° angle.

2 Holding ribbon in left hand and the folded tail in the right, roll the fold firmly in a clockwise direction for three turns to form the centre of the rose.

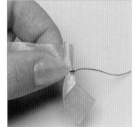

3 Still holding firmly and using the sewing thread, take three stitches at the lower edge through all layers of ribbon. Leave needle dangling.
Completed centre.

4 First petal. With left thumb and forefinger, fold the top edge of the ribbon back and down.

5 Wrap the folded ribbon once around the centre to form the petal.

6 Pick up the dangling needle and stitch through all layers of ribbon at the base of the rose.

7 Pull the thread through firmly. Work a second stitch through all layers. Leave needle dangling.

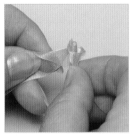

8 Second petal. With the left thumb and forefinger, fold the top edge of the ribbon back and down as before.

9 Wrap the folded ribbon once around the centre to form the second petal.

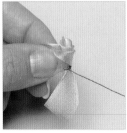

10 Pulling the thread firmly, work two stitches through all layers at the base of the rose to secure the second petal.

11 Remaining petals. Continue folding, wrapping and stitching as for steps 4-10 until the rose is the desired size (approx 2-3 more rounds).

12 Final petal. Cut off excess ribbon leaving a tail of approx 2cm (¾"). Fold the ribbon back and down as before.

13 Wrap the ribbon to form a partial petal.

14 **Securing the rose.** Turn the rose upside down. Pulling firmly, take two stitches through the base to secure and end off the thread.

15 Trim excess ribbon as close as possible to the base of the rose without cutting the stitching, approx 2-3mm (⅛").

16 **Completed rose.**

FOLDED RIBBON ROSEBUD

Folded rosebuds are worked in a similar manner to the roses. The centre of the bud is identical to the centre of the rose but only one petal is formed to complete the bud.

1 **Centre.** Fold the right hand end of the ribbon over at a 90° angle (refer to step 1 on the opposite page).

2 Holding ribbon in left hand and folded tail in right hand, roll ribbon firmly for 3 turns. Secure as for folded rose (refer to step 3 on opposite page).

3 **Petal.** With the left thumb and forefinger, fold the top edge of the ribbon back and down.

4 Wrap the ribbon in an anti-clockwise direction, allowing the folded edge to angle towards the base of the bud.

5 Stitch through all layers to secure. End off the thread. Trim the excess ribbon close to the stitching.

6 **Completed folded ribbon roses and rosebuds.**

FOUR-LEGGED KNOT STITCH

Four-legged knot stitch has the appearance of a cross with a knot in the centre. The knots can be worked close together or sprinkled randomly. Note: A cross was marked and the base stitches were worked longer for photographic purposes only.

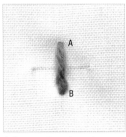

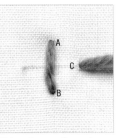

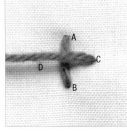

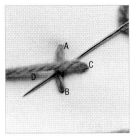

1 Secure thread on the back. Bring needle to front at A at the top of a cross. Take thread to back at B to form the first stitch.

2 Bring the needle to the front at C and pull the thread through.

3 Lay the thread from C to D, and hold in position with the thumb (thumb not shown).

4 With the thread looped below, slide the needle from the upper right to the lower left under both threads at the centre.

5 Pull the thread through gently, ensuring the loop is under the tip of the needle.

6 Continue to pull through to tighten the knot.

7 Take needle to the back at D.

8 Pull the thread through and secure on the back. **Completed four-legged knot stitch.**

Hints for left-handed embroiderers

1 For most stitches, work from right to left (or the opposite direction to right handers' instructions).

2 Most stitches are worked as a mirror image to the way right handers work them. When following instructions pretend you are looking into a mirror rather than copying exactly what you see. If taking a class, sit in front of the teacher rather than alongside.

3 Some instructions are easier to follow if you turn them upside down.

4 When wrapping, twisting or looping the thread, do it in the opposite direction to that in the instructions for right handers.

5 Stitches that are worked from top to bottom for right handers are also worked from top to bottom for left handers.

FRENCH KNOT

A French knot is a raised stitch. The traditional French knot was worked with only one wrap, however today it is often worked with more. A larger knot will look neater worked with more strands of thread rather than too many wraps.

1 Secure the thread on the back of the work. Bring the thread to the front.

2 Hold thread firmly with left thumb and index finger 3cm (1¼") away from the fabric.

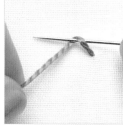

3 With left hand, bring thread over the needle. Ensure the needle points away from the fabric.

4 Wrap thread around the needle. Keeping the thread taut, begin to turn the point of the needle towards the fabric.

5 Take the needle to the back approx 1–2 fabric threads away from the emerging thread.

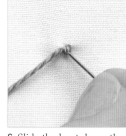

6 Slide the knot down the needle onto the fabric. Pull the thread until the knot is firmly around the needle.

7 Slowly push the needle to the back of the fabric while holding the knot in place under your thumb. Begin to pull the thread through.

8 Continue to pull until the thread disappears under your thumb and is completely pulled through. **Completed French knot.**

Hints on knot stitches

Knotted embroidery stitches have a wonderful textural quality that makes you want to reach out and touch them.

All the individual stitches offer something a little different – from the flatness of a Chinese knot through to the pebbly French and Danish knots and the fluffy Ghiordes knot. Single knot stitches are quite tiny and are not often used alone, although, entire designs can be worked using only one type of knot.

1 To provide a strong foundation for closely worked knots, use firm hardwearing fabric for the work.

2 Work each stitch by stabbing the needle through the fabric.

3 It is easier to work some knots with the fabric in a hoop. This leaves your hands free to position stitches and manipulate loops or to wrap the thread around the needle.

FRENCH KNOT – RIBBON FLOWER

Ribbon French knot flowers are created by working a loose French knot with ribbon and then anchoring this with a firm French knot using thread.

1 **Petals.** Use a length of ribbon approx 30cm (12") long. Bring ribbon to front at A, leaving a short tail, approx 1cm (⅜") on the back.

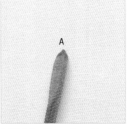

2 Holding the ribbon in the left hand, place the needle under the ribbon approx 1.5cm (⅝") away from A.

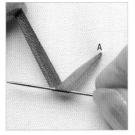

3 Holding the ribbon in the left hand, take the ribbon behind the needle towards A.

4 With the left hand, take the ribbon over the needle, forming one wrap.

5 Place the needle in the fabric very close to A, allowing the wrap to slide gently down the needle onto the fabric. **Do not pull the knot tight.**

6 Begin to pull the ribbon through gently.

7 Continue pulling ribbon through gently, leaving a very loose French knot on the fabric. Leave the ribbon dangling on the back.

8 **Centre.** Thread a needle with a thread and secure on the back. Bring to the front in the centre of the ribbon French knot.

9 Pull thread through. Work a French knot in centre. Take thread to back. Trim ribbon to 1cm (⅜") and secure tail with thread. **Completed flower.**

10 **Ribbon French knot flowers, with and without thread French knot centres.**

GATHERED ROSE

To make this superb rose, two widths of ribbon are stitched together, gathered and couched in a spiral to the fabric.

We used two 46cm (18") lengths of silk ribbon.

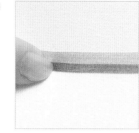

1 Cut one 46cm (18") length of 7mm (⁵⁄₁₆") ribbon. Cut a piece of 4mm (³⁄₁₆") ribbon the same length. Place ribbons together so they match along one edge.

2 Using machine sewing thread, work a tiny running stitch through both ribbons close to the edge at which the ribbons match.

3 Pull up the running stitch to gather the ribbons until they measure 23cm (9"). Leave the needle and thread dangling.

4 At the end with the dangling thread, fold the corner down diagonally to meet gathered edge. Using the dangling thread, secure with two tiny stitches.

5 Using the same thread, position this end in the centre of shape to be filled. Couch in place with a tiny stitch just through the edge of the ribbons.

6 Begin folding the ribbons around the centre. Couch in place at 3-4mm (⅛-³⁄₁₆") intervals using tiny stitches.

7 Continue spiralling the ribbon ensuring the gathers are even. Couch in place as you go until all the ribbon is attached. Place last stitch very close to end.

8 At the end, fold the top edge of the wider ribbon down diagonally. Attach it to the fabric with two tiny stitches.

9 Take the thread to the back and end off.
Completed gathered rose.

10 **Gathered roses are used along with other techniques to create this eye-catching floral display.**

79

GHIORDES KNOT

This easy stitch is also known as Turkey work or single knot tufting. It is a series of very closely worked loops, cut and trimmed as required. The cut loops are often combed and fluffed out. This stitch is particularly effective when worked in wool. Mark the fabric with dots as indicated.

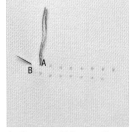

1 **First row.** Take needle to back at A. Pull the thread through, leaving a long tail on the front. Re-emerge at B a short distance from A.

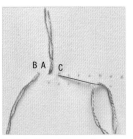

2 Pull thread through, taking care not to pull the tail through the fabric. With the thread below the needle, take the needle to the back at C.

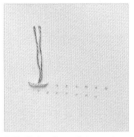

3 Pull the thread through the fabric to the back, forming the first back stitch.

4 Bring the needle to the front at A. Take care not to catch the thread of the back stitch.

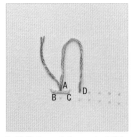

5 Pull thread through. With thread above, take the needle to the back at D, forming the first loop. The loop is the same length as the tail of thread.

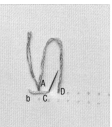

6 Hold the loop and tail flat on the fabric under the thumb (thumb not shown). Bring the needle to the front at C.

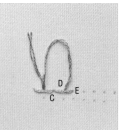

7 With the thread below, take the needle to the back at E. Pull thread through. This forms the second back stitch.

8 Continue until required number of loops have been formed. Ensure the final stitch is a back stitch. Leave a tail of thread on the front.

9 **Completed first row. Second row.** Bring the needle to the front at F below A to begin the second row of Ghiordes knots.

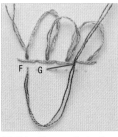

10 Take the needle to the back at G to form the first back stitch on the second row.

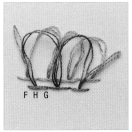

11 Bring needle to front at H to form first loop on second row. Continue until required number of loops are formed.

12 **Trimming loops.** Cut all loops. Smooth the loops out between fingers and trim evenly to desired length.

GLOVE STITCH

Traditionally used in the making of fine kid gloves, this stitch is similar in appearance to the first row of zigzag stitch. It is often used to stitch the edges of chatelaines and boxes together as it makes a very pretty edge. Marking two parallel lines on the fabric will help to keep the stitches even.

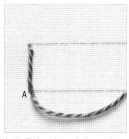

1 Bring the thread to the front at A and take it to the back at B.

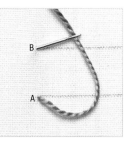

2 Pull the thread through to form a vertical straight stitch. Re-emerge at A through the same hole in the fabric.

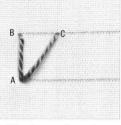

3 Take the needle to the back at C. Pull the thread through to form a diagonal straight stitch.

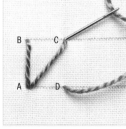

4 Bring the thread to the front at D, directly below C. Take the needle to the back at C through the same hole in the fabric.

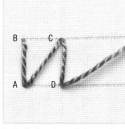

5 Pull the thread through. Re-emerge at D through the same hole in the fabric.

6 Continue in the same manner for the required distance ending on a vertical stitch. **Completed glove stitch.**

GRAB STITCH WITH RIBBON BUD

Grab stitch can be used to form the stem and calyx on buds. It needs to be worked in association with a stitch such as ribbon stitch. Here it is worked using six strands of thread.

1 Bring the thread to the front. Take the needle back through the ribbon selvedge, next to where it came up, without going through the fabric.

2 Take the needle under the ribbon and up through the selvedge on the left side. Pull the thread through leaving the loop that is formed.

3 Take the needle through the loop. Holding the ribbon bud with left thumb, pull the grab stitch tight towards left side (thumb not shown).

4 **Stem.** Anchor the stitch by taking the needle to the back of the fabric approx 1cm (⅜") away from the base of the bud. **Completed bud with grab stitch calyx and stem.**

GRANITOS

These tiny stitches are quick and easy to do. They can create different effects depending on the number of stitches worked and the thread used. Each granitos is worked using the same two holes in the fabric.

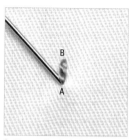

1 First stitch. Bring the needle to the front at A. Pull the thread through and take it to the back of the fabric at B.

2 Second stitch. Bring the needle to the front at A, taking care to emerge through the same hole in the fabric as the previous stitch.

3 Pull the thread through. Loop the thread to the left and take the needle to the back at B (through the same hole in the fabric).

4 Gently pull thread through, ensuring the stitch is positioned to the left of the first stitch.

5 Third stitch. Bring the thread to the front at A. Loop the thread to the right and take the needle to the back at B.

6 Gently pull thread through, placing stitch to the right of the previous stitches. Work a fourth stitch, positioning it to the left. **Completed granitos.**

HEM STITCH – ANTIQUE

Antique hem stitch is worked from right to left on the wrong side of the fabric. Hemstitching is worked in a similar way, but on the right side of the fabric. This drawn thread stitch is both pretty and functional as it secures the hem while providing decoration.

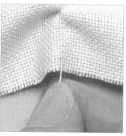

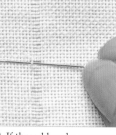

1 Drawing the threads. Using a pin, carefully ease one vertical thread from the fabric near the raw edge.

2 Very gently pull the thread, drawing it from the fabric. The fabric will gather as you pull.

3 If thread breaks, remove the broken piece. Ease remaining end out of the weave and continue drawing out the thread.

4 Draw out several adjacent threads until the band is the required depth.

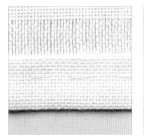

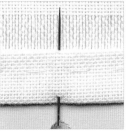

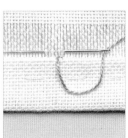

5 Preparing the hem.
Fold and press a double hem. Align the folded hem edge with the edge of the band of drawn threads. Tack in place.

6 Hemstitching. Take the needle between the two layers of the hem, a short distance away from the upper fold. Emerge on the upper fold.

7 Pull the end of the thread between the layers of fabric. Work a tiny back stitch to secure the thread.

8 Take needle from right to left behind the fabric threads. Collect required number of threads onto needle. Bring needle to the front.

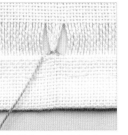

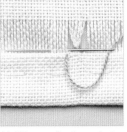

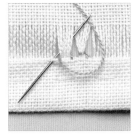

9 Pull thread through. Take the needle from right to left behind the bundle of threads. Re-emerge below the last thread in bundle, just catching the hem.

10 Pull the thread firmly until the bundle of threads is tightly grouped together. **Completed first stitch.**

11 Take needle through the hole that has been formed, to right side of fabric. Collect the same number of threads onto the needle as for the first stitch.

12 Pull thread through. Take needle from right to left behind the bundle of threads. Re-emerge below the last thread in bundle, just catching the hem.

13 Pull the thread firmly until the bundle of threads is tightly grouped together. **Completed second stitch.**

14 Continue working stitches following steps 11-13.

15 To finish off, work a tiny back stitch close to the fold just below the last bundle.

16 Completed antique hem stitch on the right side of the fabric.

HEM STITCH – SERPENTINE

Also known as trellis hem stitch. It can be worked on either the right or wrong side of the fabric. Always bundle an even number of threads in the first row in order to have the same number when you divide in the second row. For drawing out the threads, see page 82.

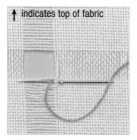

↑ indicates top of fabric

1 Starting on the left hand edge, secure the thread with a tiny back stitch on the wrong side.

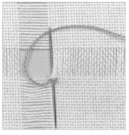

2 Take a tiny vertical stitch emerging below edge of drawn thread area. Count an even number of threads to the right of this stitch (usually 4, 6, 8 or 10).

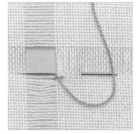

3 Take the needle from right to left behind the counted fabric threads. Bring the needle tip to the front.

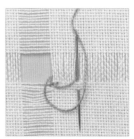

4 Pull the thread through. Take needle to back just to the right of the last thread. Re-emerge directly below in the fabric.

5 Pull the thread firmly until the bundle of threads is tightly grouped together. **Completed first stitch.**

6 Take the needle from right to left behind the same number of threads as for the first stitch. Bring the needle tip to the front.

7 Pull the thread through. Take needle to the back just to the right of the last thread. Re-emerge directly below in the fabric.

8 Pull the thread firmly until the bundle of threads is tightly grouped together. **Completed second stitch.**

9 Following steps 6–8, continue to the end of the row.

10 Turn fabric upside down. Secure the thread to the fabric as in step 1. Work a hem stitch, picking up half the number of threads only from first bundle.

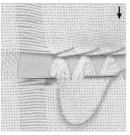

11 Take needle behind fabric threads, picking up half the number of threads from the sec-ond bundle and the remaining threads from the first bundle.

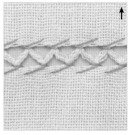

12 Complete the stitch as for steps 4-5. Continue working, re- grouping threads in the bundles. **Completed serpentine hem stitch.**

HERRINGBONE STITCH

Also known as plaited stitch and catch stitch. It is often used to work decorative borders. Mark two parallel lines to help keep your stitches even. Space the stitches closer or wider apart according to the desired effect.

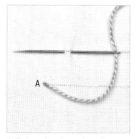 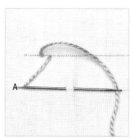  

1 Bring the thread to front at A. With the thread below needle, take the needle from right to left on the upper line, approx 6mm (¼") to the right of A. Pick up approx 2mm(¹⁄₁₆") of fabric.

2 Pull the thread through. With thread above needle take the needle from right to left for 2mm (¹⁄₁₆") on the lower line, approx 1cm (³⁄₈") to the right of A.

3 Pull the thread through. With thread below the needle, pick up 2mm (¹⁄₁₆") of fabric on the upper line (the same distance as before).

4 Continue working evenly spaced stitches, alternating bet- ween the lower and upper lines. **Completed herringbone stitch.**

HERRINGBONE STITCH – DOUBLE

Also known as Indian herringbone stitch. This stitch is formed from two rows of herringbone. A second row using the same spacing is worked over the first, interlacing the stitches together. Using contrasting coloured threads highlights the decorative effect of the interlacing.

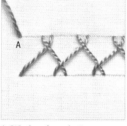 

1 Work a foundation row of herringbone stitch. Bring a second thread to the front at A, directly above the beginning of the previous row.

2 Take the needle from right to left on the lower line (between the stitches of the previous row). Pick up approximately 2mm (¹⁄₁₆") of fabric.

  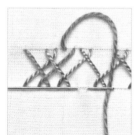 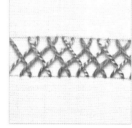

3 Pull the thread through. Take the needle under the second diagonal stitch of the previous row. The needle does not go through the fabric.

4 Pull the thread through. Picking up 2mm (¹⁄₁₆") of fabric as before, take the needle from right to left between the stitches on the upper line.

5 Pull the thread through. Take the needle from right to left on the lower line. The thread will cross over the diagonal stitch on the foundation row.

6 Continue working stitches, weaving the thread under or over the diagonal stitches in the foundation row. **Completed double herringbone stitch.**

HOLBEIN STITCH

Also known as double running stitch. This stitch is created in two stages. Work one row of evenly spaced running stitches and then a second row to fill the remaining spaces in the first row. Worked carefully, this stitch is identical on the front and back. We used two thread colours for photographic purposes.

1 Bring the thread to the front at the right hand end of the line to be covered.

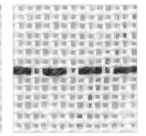

2 Count two fabric threads to the left. Take the needle to the back through the next hole. Pull through and re-emerge two fabric threads further to the left.

3 Continue in this manner to the end of the line, leaving two fabric threads between each stitch.

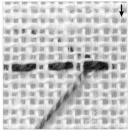

4 Turn fabric upside down. Working from right to left again, bring thread to front through same hole in fabric as left hand end of previous running stitch.

5 Take the needle to the back at end of the next running stitch. Use the same hole in the fabric and take the needle through just above thread.

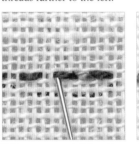

6 Re-emerge at left hand end of the stitch. Use the same hole in the fabric and bring needle through just below thread.

7 Continue in this manner, ensuring the second stitch is slightly angled. This is important for achieving a smooth line. **Completed Holbein stitch.**

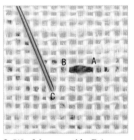

8 **Working motifs.** Bring thread to front at top right corner (A). Take to back two threads to the left (B). Count two threads across and two down. Re-emerge at C.

9 Pull thread through. Take the needle to the back two threads across and two threads up (D). Re-emerge two fabric threads to the left (E).

10 Pull through. Take the needle to the back two threads directly below (F).

11 Continue to work stitches following the design carefully, until you are one stitch from the starting point (G).

12 Stitch in the reverse direction, following steps 5-7, to complete the motif outline.

LAID WORK

Laid work is a useful method to cover large areas. It is a technique often used in goldwork where the maximum amount of expensive gold thread remains on the front. Always work on a strong, firm fabric and use a hoop.

In laid work a combination of stitches are worked, one over the other, to add texture to the shape.

This example is worked with a foundation of split stitch and satin stitch padding. A layer of couched diagonal trellis completes the design.

1 Foundation. Draw a shape. Work the outline using split stitch (see page 120). Bring the thread to right side at A (outside the split stitch).

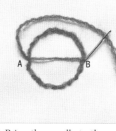

2 Take the needle to the back at B on the opposite side of the shape to work the first long stitch.

3 Bring the needle to the front of the work just above A and take to the back just above B.

4 Continue filling upper half. Keep stitches very close (no fabric shows). Take thread to back and weave under the stitches on the back to begin the lower half.

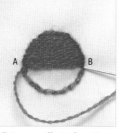

5 Bring needle to front just below A. Take the needle to the back just below B. Work lower half of the shape to complete the foundation.

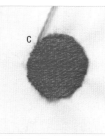

6 Trellis. Change to a new colour. Bring thread to front at C to begin working the long diagonal stitches for the trellis work.

7 Take the needle to the back of the work at D.

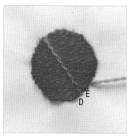

8 Bring the needle to the front at E approx 4mm (³⁄₁₆") above D. The trellis stitches will be spaced approx 4mm (³⁄₁₆") apart.

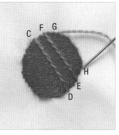

9 Pull the thread through. Take needle to back at F. Pull the thread through. Continue working trellis (G to H).

10 Weave thread on the back and emerge 4mm (³⁄₁₆") below C to begin second half. **Completed first layer of trellis.**

11 The top layer of trellis is worked in the same manner, placing the stitches at right angles to the first layer. **Completed trellis.** (cont on p.88)

12 Couching. Work through all layers. Change thread, bring to front close to a trellis intersection. Take needle to back over intersection.

13 Pull the thread through. **First completed couching stitch.**

14 Continue couching the inter-sections working one row at a time.

15 **Completed laid work.**

LONG AND SHORT STITCH

This filling stitch is very useful for a gradual shading of colour.

1 Place the fabric in a hoop. Outline the shape to be filled, using split stitch. This helps to create a neat edge.

2 **First row of stitches.** Bring the thread to the front just outside the split stitch outline.

3 Take to back within shape. Work a row of straight stitches, alternating a long stitch with a short stitch. Angle the stitches slightly to follow the shape.

4 **Second row of stitches.** Bring the needle to the front at A. Take it to the back close to the first stitch of the first row (splitting the stitch if necessary).

5 Bring the needle to the front at B. Take it to the back close to a stitch in the first row.

6 Continue working across the row, varying the length of the stitches and staggering their starting positions.

7 While stitches are kept as parallel as possible to each other, they may need to be angled slightly to suit the shape. Do this as gradually as possible.

8 Continue until the entire shape is filled and the outline is completely hidden. **Completed long and short stitch.**

LOOP STITCH – DAISY

This delicate loop stitch daisy is worked using 4mm (³⁄₁₆") wide silk ribbon. Work the first three petals of the daisy in a 'Y' (upside down) to ensure the petals are correctly angled. Stitch the ribbon loop petals first, then secure with tiny straight stitches. Work a French knot in the centre.

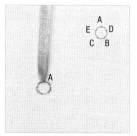

1 **Petals.** Mark a circle approx 3mm (⅛") in diameter for the centre of the flower. Bring the ribbon to the front at A.

2 Hold ribbon flat under left thumb. Place needle under the ribbon at base. Using slight upward pressure, move needle towards thumb to flatten ribbon.

3 Keeping the left thumb on the ribbon, fold it over and back towards the centre to form a loop.

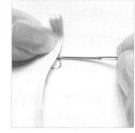

4 Reposition the thumb to hold both layers of ribbon. Take the needle to the back next to A.

5 Gently pull the ribbon through until a loop of approx 1cm (⅜") is formed. **Completed first petal.**

6 Keeping the left thumb over the loop to prevent it pulling through, bring the ribbon to the front at B (thumb not shown).

7 Form a second loop by following steps 2-5. **Completed second petal.**

8 Keeping thumb on second loop, bring the ribbon to the front at C (thumb not shown). Form a loop in the same manner. **Completed third petal.**

9 Repeat at D and E to form the fourth and fifth petals. End off the ribbon by weaving through the work on the back.

10 **Securing Petals.** Using thread, bring it to front just below A. Take a tiny stitch, 2mm (¹⁄₁₆") long, over the petal. Take the needle through all layers.

11 Repeat for the remaining four petals.

12 Work a French knot in the centre. **Completed loop stitch daisy.**

LOOP STITCH–DAFFODIL

 The centre of each daffodil is made from a spiral of gathered ribbon. Each of the seven petals is a carefully folded and couched loop stitch. Both parts of the flower are created from 7 mm (⁵⁄₁₆") wide silk ribbon. 4mm (³⁄₁₆") wide ribbon is used to couch the petals in place.

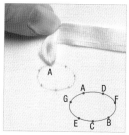

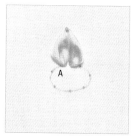

1 Mark an oval. Bring wide ribbon to the front at A. Lay ribbon flat. Form a mitre by carefully folding the ribbon under 1.5cm (⅝") away from A.

2 Using a narrow, darker shade of ribbon, work a tiny straight stitch at the tip to hold the petal in place. Leave this ribbon dangling on the back.

3 Keeping the ribbon flat, form a mitre again by folding it over towards the centre.

4 Place thumb over ribbon to hold in place. Ensuring there are no twists, take it to the back 5mm (¼") to the right of A. **Completed first petal.**

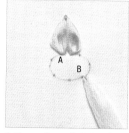

5 **Second petal.** Bring the ribbon to the front at B on the marked oval.

6 Following steps 1-4, complete the second petal.

7 Work five more petals in the same manner at the positions indicated on the diagram. End off the ribbons on the back. **Completed petals.**

8 **Centre.** Using a different colour, cut a length of wide ribbon 25cm (10") long. Bring to the front in the centre of the oval.

9 Using matching thread and starting from the end nearest the fabric, work running stitch (see page 107) along one edge of the ribbon.

10 Gather up to 10cm (4"). Leave the thread dangling. Wrap gathered ribbon once clockwise around centre. Using a second thread couch ribbon in place.

11 Continue spiralling gathered ribbon, couching as you wrap until the centre of the daffodil is filled (approx 2½ rounds). Take end of ribbon to back.

12 Ensuring the gathers are pulled up, secure the end of the ribbon with the dangling thread. End off threads. **Completed daffodil.**

LOOP STITCH – FLOWER

This flower is formed by working a loose loop of ribbon and anchoring it to the fabric with a French knot. The French knot is pulled tightly so that the sides of the ribbon fold freely, giving fullness to the flowers. We used 7mm (⁵⁄₁₆") wide silk ribbon for the petals and stranded thread for the French knot.

1 **Petals.** Bring the ribbon to the front at A, leaving a short tail, approx 1cm (⅜") on the back of the fabric.

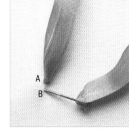

2 Take the needle to the back at B, approx 2-3mm (⅛") below A.

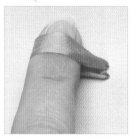

3 To keep the ribbon from twisting, place a finger in the loop and begin to pull the ribbon through gently.

4 Take finger out of loop and continue pulling until the loop measures approx 1cm (⅜"). Leave needle and ribbon dangling. **Completed petals.**

5 **Centre.** Thread a crewel nee-dle with stranded thread. Secure on the back. Flatten ribbon loop so centre of loop meets fabric at C, halfway between A and B.

6 Hold the loop in place. Bring the needle to the front at C.

7 Still holding the loop, pull the needle through.

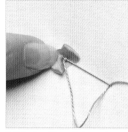

8 Work a French knot in the centre, pulling it tightly to allow the two sides of the ribbon to fold freely.

9 Trim ribbon on back to 1cm (⅜") and secure with thread. **Completed loop stitch flower.**

10 Loop stitch flowers worked using 2 widths of ribbon.

LOOP STITCH – TWISTED PLUMES

This variation of loop stitch creates an elegant slender plant. These loop stitch plumes are worked along a vertical line with 7 mm (⅜") wide silk ribbon.

Mark the line onto the fabric for the required length of the plume.

In loop stitch the ribbon is folded to the front of the emerging ribbon with both sides of the loop aligned. For twisted loop stitch the ribbon is folded behind and alternately from left to right.

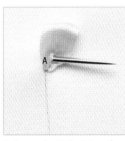

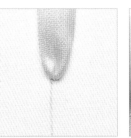

1 Flower tip. Bring the ribbon to the front at the top of the line. Lay the ribbon upwards and flat on the fabric.

2 With a finger on the ribbon, fold the ribbon over the finger. Ensure there are no twists in the ribbon.

3 Take the needle to the back just below the emerging ribbon. Gently pull through, leaving a 1cm (⅜") loop. Remove finger as loop tightens.

4 Second stitch. Bring the needle to the front through the base of the first stitch at A.

5 Pull through. Fold the ribbon to the right and under.

6 Placing your thumb on the fold, take needle to back approx 5mm (¼") below A (thumb not shown). Pull through leaving a loop. **Completed second stitch.**

7 Third stitch. Bring the needle to the front through the base of the previous stitch.

8 Pull the ribbon through. Fold the ribbon to the left and under.

9 Placing thumb on fold as before, take needle to back approx 5mm (¼") below start of the stitch. Pull ribbon through leaving a loop. **Completed third stitch.**

10 Continue working stitches in the same manner, alternating from right to left to the end of the line. **Completed twisted loop stitch plume.**

NEEDLEWEAVING – BAR

Needlewoven bars are most often used in needlelace and stumpwork. In flower or fruit embroidery, they make lovely sepals or tiny leaves. Each needlewoven bar is detached from the fabric. It can then be gently manipulated and anchored to the fabric to give the desired effect.

1 Securely anchor the thread on the back. Bring the thread to front at A and take to back at B, leaving a loop of thread approx 7mm (⁵⁄₁₆") long on the front.

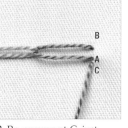

2 Re-emerge at C, just below A taking care not to pull the loop through. Pass a piece of waste thread through the loop.

3 With your left hand, hold the waste thread taut, slightly above the surface of the work. Continue to hold this taut while you work.

4 Weave the needle over the lower thread of the loop and under the upper thread. Do not pierce the fabric.

5 Pull the thread through firmly and push the wrap down onto the fabric with the tip of the needle.

6 Weave the needle over the upper thread and under the lower thread. Do not pierce the fabric.

7 Pull through firmly and push the wrap down the loop with the tip of the needle so it sits snugly against the first wrap.

8 Continue working steps 4-7, weaving the stitches over and under the threads of the loop. Push each wrap firmly against the previous one.

9 Continue weaving until the loop is completely filled and the wraps are firmly packed.

10 Remove the waste thread. Take the needle to the back approx 5mm (¼") away from A.

11 Pull the thread through. The bar slightly curves and does not lie flat against the fabric. **Completed needlewoven bar.**

12 The green sepals below the raspberries are formed with needlewoven bars.

NEEDLEWEAVING – OPEN BASE PICOT

This picot is a lace-making technique used in stumpwork to create raised embroidery. The picot is worked around a pin inserted in the fabric and is only attached to the fabric at one end. Beautiful picots depend on even tension and tightly packed stitches.

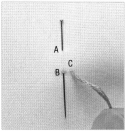

1 Foundation threads. Insert a long pin from A to B for approx 1cm (⅜"). This is the picot length. Bring the thread to the front at C and pull through.

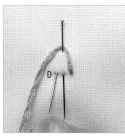

2 Wrap the thread anti-clockwise under the head of the pin. Insert the needle at D.

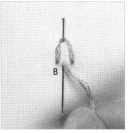

3 Pull the thread through. Re-emerge just to the right of B. Pull the thread through.

4 Wrap the thread clockwise around the head of the pin. The centre thread crosses the pin and becomes the third foundation thread.

5 Hold the thread taut to the right. Give a firm tug.

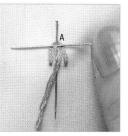

6 Towards the top of the pin (A) weave the needle from right to left under the foundation threads (over, under, over).

7 Pull the thread through.

8 Pull the thread firmly up against the pin.

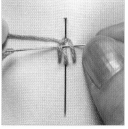

9 Hold thread taut to left, weave needle from left to right (under, over, under) the foundation stitches. You may find it easier to turn the work slightly to do this.

10 Pull the thread through until the loop is snug against the first foundation thread.

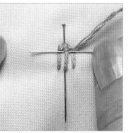

11 Weave the needle from the right to the left under the centre thread. Push needle up towards the top of the picot. Pack the threads as tightly as possible.

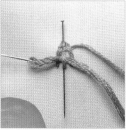

12 Begin to pull the thread through.

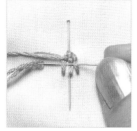

13 Before thread is completely through, place point of needle in the loop being formed. (This helps to maintain the shape, keeping outer line of foundation threads even).

14 Weave from left to right, slid-ing needle under, over, under (step 9). Continue weaving towards base of picot, packing firmly each left-to-right row.

15 Continue weaving until the foundation threads are firmly packed. Take the needle to the back at the base of the picot (close to C).

16 Pull through and end off on the wrong side. Remove the pin. **Completed picot.** The picot can now be twisted and man-ipulated into shape.

NEEDLEWEAVING – CLOSED BASE PICOT

This picot features a narrow, closed base.

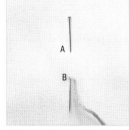

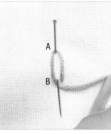

1 Insert a long pin from A to B, for approx 1cm (⅜"). This is the picot length. Bring the thread to the front at the right of the pin.

2 Wrap the thread in an anti-clockwise direction around the pinhead at A and under the tip at B. Keep the loop plump (do not pull too tightly).

3 Take thread diagonally across pin and wrap it clockwise around the pinhead. There are now three foundation threads around the pin.

4 Begin weaving. Slide the needle from the right to the left under the centre thread (over, under, over).

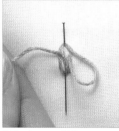

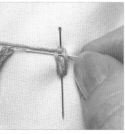

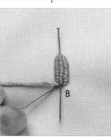

5 Begin to pull the thread through.

6 Pull the thread through firmly against the pin. Weave the needle from the left to right (under, over, under).

7 Pull the thread through. Continue weaving, packing each row firmly as you work towards the base. To end off, take needle to the back close to B.

8 Remove the pin. **Completed closed base needleweaving picot.**

95

NET STITCH

Net stitch is completely detached from the fabric except at the beginning and end of a row. It requires a stitch such as blanket stitch for the first row of stitching. Each row uses a continuous length of thread and is worked from the same side of the shape. Couch a cord at the top of the shape for the foundation.

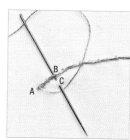

1 **Blanket stitch.** Start at one end of cord. Use a new thread. Bring needle to front at A. Take a small stitch from B to C. The thread is under the needle.

2 Pull the thread through. **Com- pleted first blanket stitch.**

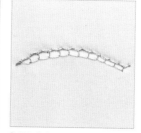

3 Work loose blanket stitches to the end of the row, taking one stitch between each couching stitch. Take the needle to the back and end off.

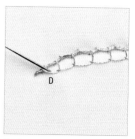

4 **First row of net stitch.** Using a new thread, bring the needle to the front at D on the left side of the work.

5 With the thread under the needle, take the needle through the loop of the second blanket stitch. Do not go through fabric.

6 Pull thread through until the stitch wraps loosely around the centre of the blanket stitch loop.

7 Again, with the thread under the needle, take the needle through the loop of the third blanket stitch.

8 Pull the thread through in the same manner as before. Continue to the end of the row. Take the needle to the back at E.

9 Pull the thread through and end off. **Second row.** Using a new thread and starting on the left side of the work, bring the needle to the front at F.

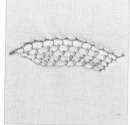

10 Continue to the end of the row. Continue working rows from left to right for the required shape using a new thread for each row.

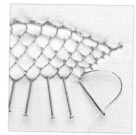

11 To secure final row, stretch net and hold in place with pins. Using new thread, work a tiny stitch through fabric at first pin, catching loop of net stitch.

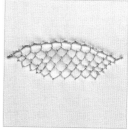

12 Continue until all loops of final row are anchored to fabric. **Completed net stitch shape.** For straight sides, add a net stitch at start and end of each row.

OUTLINE STITCH

This stitch is very similar to stem stitch and is worked in a similar way. The difference is in the position of the thread. In outline stitch the thread is always kept above the needle.

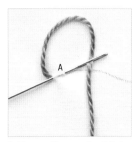

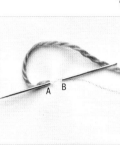

1 Draw a line on the fabric. Bring the needle to the front at the left end of the line. With the thread above the needle, take the needle to the back at A and re-emerge at the end.

2 Pull the thread through. Again with the thread above the needle, take the needle from B to A. Ensure the tension is the same for each stitch.

3 Pull the thread through. Continue working stitches in the same manner. Always keep the thread above the needle and the stitches the same length.

4 To end off, take the thread to the back for the last stitch but do not re-emerge. Secure the thread on the back with tiny back stitches. **Completed outline stitch.**

Hints on wool embroidery

1 Wool embroidery can be worked onto a large variety of fabrics. However, the weave of the fabric must be able to open up so the yarn can easily pass through without wearing excessively.

2 Work with an even tension but one that is slightly looser than for other thread embroidery.

3 Ensure the fabric you are stitching on has similar care requirements as the yarn you are stitching with.

4 To avoid the yarn becoming worn, use only short lengths approximately 40cm (16") long.

5 If the ply of the yarn unravels, gently twist the yarn with your fingers to re-ply it. If the yarn appears to be over twisted, let the needle dangle freely for a few seconds and allow the yarn to settle back to its original twist.

6 Use a needle which will make a large enough hole in the fabric for the yarn to pass through easily. This will help reduce wear on the yarn. Tapestry and chenille needles are the most suitable.

7 If you find it difficult to thread the needle, twist and fold the end of the yarn over before threading it through the eye of the needle. Moistening the end may also help.

8 To secure the start and finish of the thread, weave the tail through other stitches on the back of the work.

9 If you choose to knot the end of your wool, don't trim the tail too closely. Because wool is springy, knots will fall out if they are too close to the end. A tail approximately 1cm (⅜") long will ensure the knot stays intact.

OYSTER STITCH

Oyster stitch is a combination of twisted chain and chain stitch and can be used singly or in rows. It is an excellent stitch to add texture and is also suitable for outlines and borders.

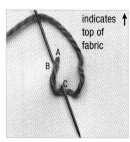

indicates ↑ top of fabric

1 **First stitch.** Bring the thread to the front at A. Take to the back at B, and re-emerge at C. Take thread under the needle tip in an anti-clockwise direction.

2 Begin to pull the thread through.

3 Pull until the loop lies firmly on the fabric.

4 Slide the needle under the right hand thread just below A. The needle does not go through the fabric.

5 Pull the thread through. Allow the thread to lie alongside the twisted chain on the fabric.

6 Take the needle to the back inside the loop and next to the twist of the twisted chain. Re-emerge at the base. Ensure thread is under the tip of the needle.

7 Pull the thread through. The second loop encircles the first loop.

8 Take the needle to the back of the fabric just beyond the last loop to anchor the stitch.

9 **Completed first oyster stitch.**

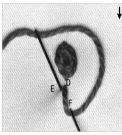

10 **Poppy.** Turn fabric upside down. Bring the needle to the front at D. Take needle from E to F and place thread under the tip of the needle as before.

11 Work the stitch following steps 2-8. Work three more stitches in the same manner to form the five petals of a poppy.

12 Fill the centre with five French knots. **Completed poppy.**

PALESTRINA STITCH

Also known as old English knot, smyrna stitch, double knot stitch and tied coral stitch. Palestrina stitch produces a line of raised knots useful for outlines or borders. It is important that the knots are evenly spaced and close together.

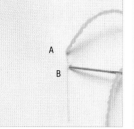

1 Draw a line on fabric. Bring needle to front at A at top of traced line. Take needle to back at B, just to the right of the line and 4mm (³⁄₁₆") away from A.

2 Bring the needle to the front at C to the left of the line and opposite B. Pull the thread through.

3 Slide the needle under the first stitch from right to left with the needle pointing upwards. Do not go through the fabric.

4 Begin to pull the thread through.

5 Continue pulling the thread through gently until the loop hugs the straight stitch.

6 Make a loop to the left.

7 Slide the needle from right to left under thread as shown. Emerge between B and C. Do not go through fabric. Ensure loop is under needle tip.

8 Gently pull the thread through forming a soft knot. **Completed first knot.**

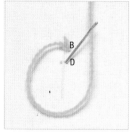

9 To begin the second stitch, take the needle to the back at D a short distance (below B) just to the right of the line.

10 Bring the needle to the front at E just to the left of the line (opposite D, below C).

11 Complete the stitch following steps 3-8.

12 Continue working stitches in the same manner. End off by taking needle to the back close to base of last stitch. **Completed Palestrina stitch.**

PIN STITCHING

Also known as point de paris. Tiny holes are created when the vertical threads of the fabric are pulled together. Tack the hem in place before beginning. Use a tapestry needle and work on the wrong side of the fabric. A firm even tension needs to be maintained on the thread throughout.

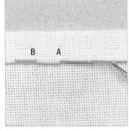

1 Take the needle through the fold of the hem at A. Slowly pull the thread through, concealing the tail of thread inside the hem.

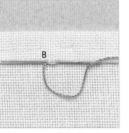

2 Work a small back stitch to secure.

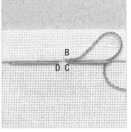

3 Take the needle from C to D on foundation fabric. C is direct-ly below B.

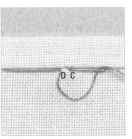

4 Firmly pull the thread through. Take the needle from C to D again, using the same holes in the fabric.

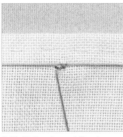

5 Pull the thread firmly to draw the threads together. A small hole will form.

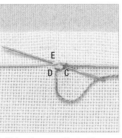

6 Take the needle to the back at C and diagonally out at E through the fold of the hem. E is directly above D.

7 Pull the thread through. **Completed first stitch.**

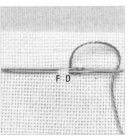

8 To begin the second stitch, take the needle to the back at D and re-emerge at F. F is approx 3mm (⅛") away from D.

9 Pull the thread through. Again, take the needle to the back at D and re-emerge at F.

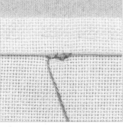

10 Firmly pull the thread through until a small hole forms.

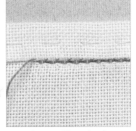

11 Take needle to back at D and then diagonally through the fold of the hem. Pull through. Continue working stitches in the same manner.

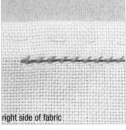

right side of fabric

12 To end off, take a backstitch in the hem fold. Run the thread through the hem for 1cm (⅜"). **Completed pin stitching.**

PISTIL STITCH

Pistil stitch is a French knot on a stem. Varying the length of the stem and the number of wraps in the knot will give different effects. Pistil stitches are often used for flower stamens and petals. For a curved effect, loosen the tension as you place the stitch for the stem.

1 Secure the thread on the back of the fabric. Bring it to the front at the base of the stitch.

2 Holding the thread firmly with the left thumb and fore- finger, wrap the thread over the needle (thumb and finger not shown).

3 Keeping the thread taut, wind it around the needle in an anti-clockwise direction for the required number of wraps.

4 Still holding the thread taut, turn the needle towards the fabric. Place the tip of the needle onto the fabric at the position for the end of the stitch.

5 Slide the wraps down the needle onto the fabric. Push the needle through the fabric, maintaining a firm tension on the thread.

6 Pull the thread through keeping the thumb over the knot. **Completed pistil stitch.**

PLUME STITCH

This stitch is most effective when worked in ribbon. Ensure the ribbon is smooth and untwisted before pulling each stitch through.

1 Take ribbon from A to B, approx 6mm (¼") away. Place a spare needle under ribbon. Pull through until a loop approx 1cm (⅜") is formed. Keep the loop tensioned with spare needle.

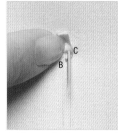

2 Flatten the loop towards the tip. Hold loop in place with left thumb or finger. Bring threaded needle to front at C, through the ribbon of the previous stitch and just above B.

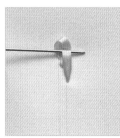

3 Pull through. Using the spare needle to control the ribbon, work the second stitch in the same manner as the first, mak-ing it approx 8mm (⁵⁄₁₆") long.

4 Continue working stitches until the line is the required length. Pull the last stitch flat against the fabric. End off ribbon on the back of the work.

RAISED CUP STITCH

aised cup stitch is a buttonhole stitch worked on a thread base. It is used in
stumpwork to create raised sections of a design. It gives a rich, textured effect.

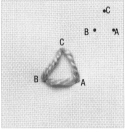

1 Base. Take a stitch from A to B. Re-emerge at C. Take to the back at A and re-emerge at B. Take to the back at C to complete the base.

2 Buttonhole stitch. Bring the needle to the front inside the triangle near A.

3 Slide the needle under base thread (the thread is to the right of the needle). Wrap thread around needle in an anti-clockwise direction.

4 Gently pull the thread through in an upward direction. A knot will form around the base stitch. **First completed buttonhole stitch.**

5 On the same base stitch, work a second buttonhole stitch in the same manner as before.

6 Continue around the triangle, working two buttonhole stitches on each base stitch. The completed round of stitches now appears circular.

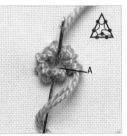

7 Begin second round of stitches at A. Slide needle under linking thread between first and second stitch of first round. Wrap thread anti-clockwise around needle.

8 Gently pull the thread through.

9 Work four more stitches. To work last stitch slide needle under linking thread between first and second stitch of second round. Wrap thread around the needle as before.

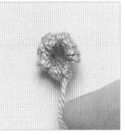

10 Gently pull the thread through.

11 To end off, take the needle to the back through the centre. Pull through to the wrong side and secure.

12 Completed raised cup.

RHODES STITCH – CIRCULAR

This variation of Rhodes stitch is worked on plain fabric and forms a circle. It is traditionally worked on canvas and forms a square. You may find it easier to gradually turn the fabric as you progress around the circle.

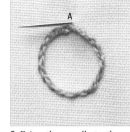

1 Draw a circle onto the right side of the fabric. Outline the circle with tiny split stitches.

2 Bring the needle to the front at the top of the circle, just out-side the split stitch outline (A).

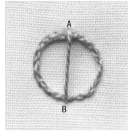

3 Pull the thread through. Take the needle to the back on the opposite side of the circle, just over the split stitch outline (B). Pull the thread through.

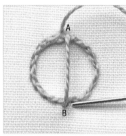

4 Re-emerge just to the left of A. Pull the thread through. Take the needle to the back just to the right of B.

5 Pull through. Continue in an anti-clockwise direction keeping the stitches close together. Ensure stitches start and finish on opposite sides.

6 Continue until the outline is covered. The last stitch lies next to the first stitch.
Completed circular Rhodes stitch.

Hints on finishing

Once the embroidery is complete it will need to be 'finished'. This may involve washing if the work has become marked from continual handling. If the fabric or threads are not suitable for washing, you may need to visit the dry cleaner. Be careful with silk fabric or thread as they have a nasty habit of not looking dirty when you finish working but marks may develop over time.

If your work needs to be washed, do this by hand using pure soap (or a detergent specially developed for this purpose, and lukewarm water. Be careful not to rub the surface of your stitching as this will cause unsightly pilling.

Rinse the work in clean water, preferably demineralised, then roll up in a clean towel and gently squeeze the excess water out. Dry quickly away from direct sunlight to keep the colours from running or fading, then press.

Pressing your embroidery can make a huge difference to the overall finish of the work. Avoid pressing the right side as this will flatten the threads too much. Make a pressing pad from a soft smooth fabric. A flannelette nappy, folded into several thicknesses, is excellent. Place the embroidery face down onto the pad and iron the back using a setting suitable for the fabric. The stitches will sink into the pad and you will be able to press the fabric flat. Steam is beneficial for silk as it increases the lustre of the thread.

THREADING RIBBON

Work with short lengths of ribbon approximately 30cm (12") long. This helps prevent the ribbon fraying and looking worn. Leave a tail approximately 1cm (⅜") long on the back of the work rather than using a knot. As you work, secure the tail with other stitches.

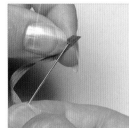

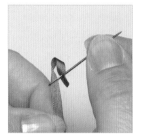

1 **Threading ribbon.** Cut end of ribbon diagonally. Thread ribbon through eye of needle. Slide needle along ribbon for approx 5cm (2").

2 Place the tip of the needle approx 6mm (¼") from the cut end of the ribbon.

3 Push the needle through the ribbon. Holding the tail in the left hand, pull needle with right hand until a knot forms at the eye of the needle.

4 The ribbon is now secured and you are ready to begin stitching.

RIBBON STITCH

Ribbon stitch, as the name suggests, is worked in ribbon only. It is worked as a straight stitch with a tightened loop at one end to anchor the ribbon. Leaves, short stems and flower petals are often worked in ribbon stitch.

1 Bring the ribbon to the front at the base of the stitch.

2 Lay the ribbon flat on the fabric. Hold in place with the left thumb just beyond the required length of the stitch.

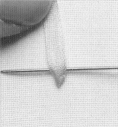

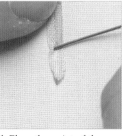

3 Place the needle under the ribbon at the base. Using a slight upward pressure, move the needle towards the thumb to spread the ribbon.

4 Place the point of the needle on the centre of the ribbon at the position for the tip of the stitch.

5 Take the needle through the ribbon and fabric to the back. Place thumb over the stitch to keep it flat and untwisted. Begin to gently pull the ribbon through.

6 Gently pull until the ribbon begins to curl along the sides. **Completed ribbon stitch.**

RIBBON STITCH – ROSE

These beautiful roses can be embroidered in both rayon and pure silk ribbon. The centres can be filled with French knots or a combination of French knots and beads. We used 12mm (½") wide rayon ribbon and a no. 24 chenille needle.

1 To mark the position of the rose on the fabric, draw a circle with a dot in the centre. Bring the ribbon to the front near the centre.

2 Lay the ribbon flat on the fabric towards the circle and hold it taut. Using a gentle tension, slide the needle under the ribbon to spread it.

3 Holding the ribbon lightly, gently raise the needle so the ribbon makes a small hill.

4 Hold the raised piece of ribbon with the left thumb. Take the needle through the centre of the ribbon and to the back on the marked circle.

5 Carefully pull the ribbon through until the end begins to curl.

6 Bring the ribbon to the front on the opposite side of the dot. Lay the ribbon towards the opposite side of the circle. Spread and raise as before.

7 Take the needle through the ribbon and fabric to the back on the marked circle. Gently pull the ribbon through.

8 Work two more ribbon stitches in the same manner, dividing the circle into quarters.

9 Bring the ribbon to the front between two petals close to the centre. Work a fifth ribbon stitch petal halfway between these two.

10 Stitch a sixth petal in the same manner opposite the fifth petal.

11 Work a petal in each of the two remaining gaps. **Completed petals.**

12 Stitch 2-4 French knots in the centre allowing them to sit on the base of the petals. **Completed ribbon stitch rose.**

RIBBON STITCH – WATER LILY

This pretty flower is created from a variety of materials and techniques. The petals use 7mm (⁵⁄₁₆") wide ribbon and sewing thread, and combine ribbon stitch with a laid thread. Gathered organdy ribbon and French knots fill the centre. Draw two circles on the fabric.

1 **Petals.** Bring ribbon to front on inner circle. Lay it towards outer circle. Bring thread to front just beyond outer circle on left of ribbon. Lay thread across ribbon.

2 Take ribbon-threaded needle over laid thread. Take it through ribbon and fabric on outer circle as for a ribbon stitch. The ribbon loops around the laid thread.

3 Pull the ribbon through, pulling tightly while holding the laid thread taut. **Completed first petal.**

4 On inner circle, bring ribbon to front just to right of first petal. Lay flat. The petals just touch each other. Lay thread across ribbon.

5 Work a ribbon stitch following steps 2-3.

6 Continue working petals in the same manner until the circle is complete. Approx 12 petals are required.

7 Take the thread to the back just beyond the outer circle and just to the right of the last petal. End off the thread but leave the ribbon on the back.

8 **Centre.** Cut 50cm (20") of organdy ribbon. Bring to front in centre. Using sewing thread and starting at end nearest fabric, gather one edge to 10cm (4").

9 Wrap the gathered ribbon once around the centre. Using the sewing thread, stitch the ribbon in place.

10 Continue wrapping the ribbon in a spiral and stitching it in place as you go until the inner circle is filled.

11 Take the end of the ribbon to the back. Ensure the gathers are pulled up then secure the end of the ribbon with the thread. End off thread.

12 Bring the ribbon to the front in the centre circle. Work 6-7 French knots among the folds of the gathered ribbon. **Completed water lily.**

RUNNING STITCH

Running stitch is quick and easy to work and is often used to form the foundation of other stitches such as whipped running stitch and Holbein stitch. When working on plain weave fabrics, make the stitch on the right side of the fabric slightly longer than the stitch on the wrong side.

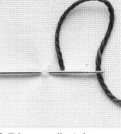

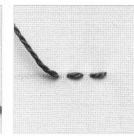

1 Draw a line on the fabric. Bring the thread to the front on the right hand end of the line.

2 Take a small stitch, skimming the needle beneath the fabric along the line.

3 Pull the thread through. Take another stitch as before, ensur-ing the stitch is the same length as the previous stitch.

4 Continue in the same manner to the end of the row. **Completed running stitch.**

RUNNING STITCH – WHIPPED

Also known as cordonnet stitch. Whipped running stitch is worked in two stages and has a raised, corded appearance. It is particularly effective when worked with two colours of thread.

1 **Foundation.** Following the step-by-step instructions above, work a line of running stitch. Keep the spaces between the stitches small.

2 **Whipping.** Change thread. Bring the thread to the front just below the centre of the first running stitch on the right hand side.

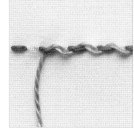

3 Take the needle from top to bottom under second stitch. To ensure needle does not go through fabric or split the stitch, pass it under, eye first.

4 Pull through using a loose tension. Take the needle from top to bottom under the third stitch.

5 Pull through. Continue to the end of the row in the same manner.

6 To end off, take the needle to the back of the fabric under the centre of the last stitch. **Completed whipped running stitch.**

SATIN STITCH

Also known as damask stitch. Satin stitch is particularly beautiful when worked with a lustrous thread such as silk or stranded cotton. Satin stitches should not be overly long or the work will appear untidy. For best results, work satin stitch in a hoop using a poke and stab technique with the needle.

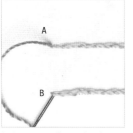

1 Straight shape. Outline the shape to be filled with split stitch.

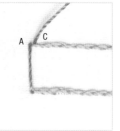

2 Bring needle to the front at A just outside the outline and pull through. Take it to the back at B on the opposite side angling the needle under the outline.

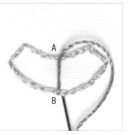

3 Pull the thread through. The stitch completely covers the outlines. Re-emerge at C very close to A and pull the thread through.

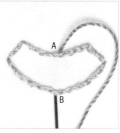

4 Take the needle to the back at D, just next to B. Pull the thread through.

5 Continue working stitches in the same manner until the shape is filled.

6 Curved shape. Starting at the centre of the shape, work a stitch from A to B. Ensure the stitch is positioned exactly at right angles to the shape at this point.

7 Pull thread through. Re-emerge very close to A and pull thread through. Take it to back near B, leaving a slightly larger space between stitches.

8 Pull thread through. Bring to front on upper edge next to last stitch. Take needle to back on lower edge, leaving a slightly larger space between stitches.

9 Continue working stitches keeping each stitch exactly at right angles to the shape. When one half of the shape is filled, take the needle to the back to finish the last stitch.

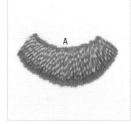

10 Slide the needle under the stitches on the back and bring to the front on the upper edge next to A. Complete the second half of the shape following steps 6-9. End off on the back.

Satin stitch worked to fill various shapes, including flowers, leaves and ribbons.

Geometric, straight and curved shapes filled with satin stitch.

SATIN STITCH – BOW WITH SPLIT STITCH OUTLINE

Split stitch is used to outline the bow. It gives a smoother, more stable edge than running stitch. It is important to angle the needle under the split stitch when coming to the front and going to the back. We used one strand of stranded silk.

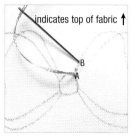

1 Draw bow outline on fabric. Secure thread with a tiny back stitch on back of fabric. **Split stitch.** Bring thread to front at A. Take a small stitch from A to B.

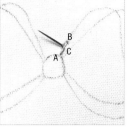

2 Bring the needle to the front at C, halfway between A and B, splitting the thread of the previous stitch.

3 Work split stitch along one traced line and then work along the second traced line to complete the right loop outline.

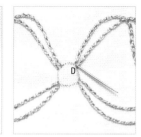

4 Work the outline of the left bow loop in the same manner. **Satin stitch.** Bring the needle to the front at D, just outside the split stitch outline.

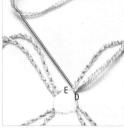

5 Take the needle to the back at E over the split stitch outline, opposite D. Angle the needle under the split stitch before taking it to the back.

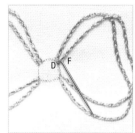

6 Pull the thread through, keep-ing an even tension. **Completed first satin stitch.** Bring the needle to the front at F, as close as possible to D.

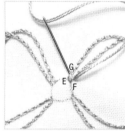

7 Take the needle to the back at G, as close as possible to E.

8 Continue stitching to the first ribbon twist keeping stitches parallel. Complete the last stitch before the twist by taking the needle to the back at H.

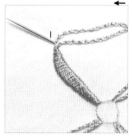

9 Rotate the fabric. Bring the needle to the front at I.

10 Pull the thread through. Take the needle to the back at H.

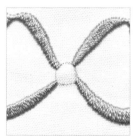

11 Continue stitching as before, rotating the fabric at each twist to complete the right loop. Complete the left bow loop in the same manner.

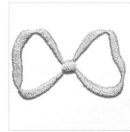

12 **Bow knot.** Work horizontal satin stitches across the bow knot. Work a layer of vertical satin stitches on top. **Completed bow.**

SATIN STITCH – PADDED

Araised effect is achieved by filling a shape with stitches such as chain, stem, seed, straight or running stitch before working the satin stitches.

1 Draw the shape on the fabric. Stitch around the outline of the shape with split or back stitch.

2 Fill the shape with the selected filling stitches, ensuring they run opposite to the direction the satin stitches will go.

3 Beginning at the widest section of the shape, cover one half with satin stitches using the stabbing technique.

4 Cover the remainder of the shape in the same manner. **Completed padded satin stitch shape.**

SATIN STITCH – PADDED BERRIES

Several layers of satin stitch can be worked to give a rounded appearance to shapes such as berries. Different stitches can be used to form the padding. In this design satin stitch has been worked. We used two shades of thread for photographic purposes only.

1 Draw the shape on the fabric. Outline the shape with split stitch. Work a square of approx-imately four vertical satin stitches in the centre.

2 Bring the needle to the front just beyond the start of the first stitch.

3 Begin to work horizontal satin stitches over the first layer. Make these stitches slightly longer than the first set of stitches.

4 Complete the layer. Begin to work a third layer making the stitches slightly longer than the previous layer. Lay the stitches across the previous ones.

5 Complete the third layer in the same manner as before. Bring the needle to the front just beyond the outline.

6 Complete the final layer, ensuring the stitches just cover the outline. Add a French knot near the centre. **Completed padded satin stitch berry.**

SCROLL STITCH

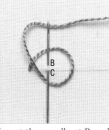

Also known as single knotted line stitch. Scroll stitch makes an attractive border. Marking a line on the fabric will help keep the stitches straight.

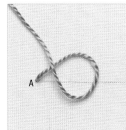

1 Secure the thread on the back. Bring the thread to the front at A. Make a loop to the right of A in a clockwise direction.

2 Insert the needle at B and re-emerge at C, taking a tiny stitch to the marked line. Ensure the circle of thread lies under both ends of the needle.

3 Pull the thread firmly so the loop tightens around the needle.

4 Pull the thread through. **Completed first stitch.**

5 Loop the thread to the right. Insert the needle from D to E. Ensure the loop is under both ends of the needle.

6 Tighten loop and pull thread through. Continue working stitches in the same manner. **Completed scroll stitch.**

SEED STITCH

Also known as speckling stitch and isolated back stitch. Seed stitch is a filling stitch. When used as a background or to fill a shape, the stitches should be scattered irregularly.

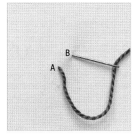

1 Bring the thread to the front at A. Take the needle to the back at B, a short distance away.

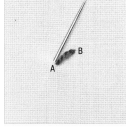

2 Pull the thread through and re-emerge next to A.

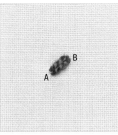

3 Pull the thread through. Take the thread to the back next to B. Pull the thread through.

4 Continue working random seed stitches in the area to be filled, varying the angle of the stitches. **Completed seed stitch.**

SHADOW WORK – DOUBLE BACK STITCH

Shadow work creates a delicate effect of shading on fine fabrics. It can be worked from either the wrong or the right side of the fabric. Here it is worked from the right side.

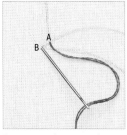

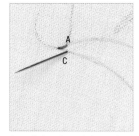

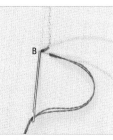

1 Begin with a waste knot. Bring needle to front at A, 1.5mm (1⁄16") away from point of shape. Pull through. Take the needle to back at B, exactly on the point.

2 Pull the thread through. Re-emerge at C, on the lower line directly below A.

3 Pull the thread through. Take the needle to the back at B using the same hole in the fabric as before.

4 Pull the thread through. Re-emerge at D, on the upper line, 1.5mm (1⁄16") away from A.

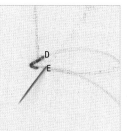

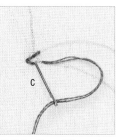

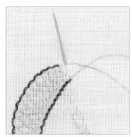

5 Pull the thread through. Take the needle to the back at A, using exactly the same hole in the fabric as before.

6 Pull the thread through and re-emerge at E on the lower line (opposite D).

7 Pull the thread through. Take needle to the back at C using the same hole in the fabric.

8 Continue working stitches in the same manner as steps 4–7. To work a curve, the stitches on the inside line are gradually reduced in length.

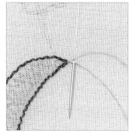

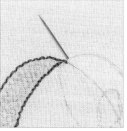

9 Crossover. To create the effect of twisting, the lower curve crosses over the upper curve. Work the first stitch of the crossover on the lower line.

10 Pull the thread through. Bring the needle to the front on the upper line for the second stitch of the crossover.

11 Take the needle to the back to the left of the intersection on the lower line.

12 Continue stitching as before. To end off or begin a new thread, weave through the threads on the wrong side, close to the edge.

SHADOW WORK – CLOSED HERRINGBONE STITCH

When shadow work is stitched with the wrong side of the fabric facing, it is known as closed herringbone stitch.

Both double back stitch and closed herringbone stitch are worked with the fabric in a hoop to help maintain an even tension.

We used a no.26 tapestry needle without a knot and one strand of silk thread. A tapestry needle parts the fabric threads rather than splitting them.

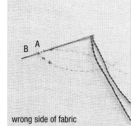

1 Draw a shape on wrong side of the fabric. On the upper line, take the needle from A to B.

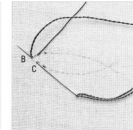

2 Pull thread through leaving a small tail approx 5cm (2") long. On lower line, take needle from C to B in the same hole.

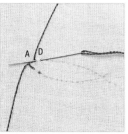

3 Pull the thread through. On the upper line take the needle to the back at D and re-emerge at A in the same hole.

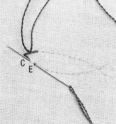

4 Pull the thread through. On the lower line take the needle from E to C in the same manner.

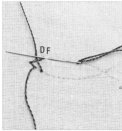

5 Pull the thread through. On the upper line take the needle from F to D in the same hole.

6 Continue closed herringbone stitch to crossover point.

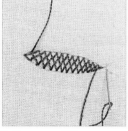

7 **Crossover.** When crossover point is reached, make sure the upper line stitch at the inter- section is worked first.

8 The lower line stitch will now cross over at the intersection. Check the right side of the fabric before proceeding.

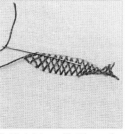

9 **Finishing off.** Weave the tails of thread under the stitches as close as possible to the edge.

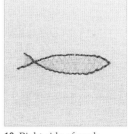

10 Right side of work. **Completed shadow work.**

SHADOW TRAPUNTO

Shadow trapunto is a form of Italian quilting. Two layers of fabric are stitched together with running stitch and the shapes filled with yarn. In this design, work the running stitches using a no.10 quilter's needle and one strand of stranded cotton and the filling with a no.20 tapestry needle and tapestry wool.

1 Trace the design onto the fabric. Using a contrasting sewing thread, tack both layers together, using long stitches in a grid formation.

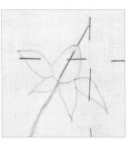

2 **Outlines.** Start with a waste knot approx 6mm (¼") away inside area to be filled. Slide needle between both layers, emerging on traced line.

3 Firmly pull the thread through so the waste knot is buried between the two layers of fabric.

4 Take needle through fabric 2mm (¹⁄₁₆") away on traced line. Re-emerge 2mm (¹⁄₁₆") away, to form the first running stitch.

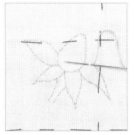

5 Pull the thread through. Continue working tiny running stitches approx 2mm (¹⁄₁₆") in length, along all traced lines of the design. End off on the back.

6 **Completed outlined design.** Remove all tacking threads.

wrong side of fabric

7 **Filling.** Turn work to wrong side. Insert needle at narrowest part of shape between the two layers. Run needle lengthwise, emerging at the end of shape.

8 Pull through gently, leaving a very short tail of approx 1mm (less than ¹⁄₁₆") extending from the fabric.

9 Cut the yarn as close as possible to the fabric.

10 Continue filling the shape, keeping the lines of yarn parallel. Use shorter lengths as necessary until the shape is filled.

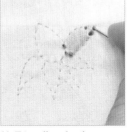

11 Trim all ends of yarn close to the fabric. Using the tip of the needle, hook the ends of yarn under the fabric.

12 Using the side of the needle, carefully stroke the fabric threads to conceal any holes.

114

right side of fabric

13 Two-tone rosebud. On the wrong side and with darker col-oured yarn, work the first filling stitch. Begin at tip of upper part of shape. Take yarn one third down the shape.

14 Continue filling the upper part of the shape with parallel lines of yarn.

15 Using lighter coloured yarn, fill in lower part of shape. Begin from opposite end, with needle re-emerging approx 2mm (¹⁄₁₆") away from the darker yarn.

16 Trim and conceal ends. **Completed shadow trapunto.**

SHEAF FILLING STITCH

Also known as faggot filling stitch. Each sheaf filling stitch is worked separately and looks like a tiny sheaf of wheat.

Any type of thread can be used, depending on the effect desired. It can be worked randomly or set in geometric patterns.

1 Secure the thread on the back. Work a vertical straight stitch.

2 Work a second vertical stitch on one side of the first stitch. Work another vertical stitch on the other side of the first stitch.

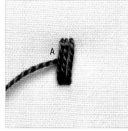

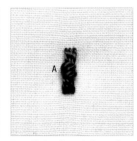

3 Bring the thread to the front at A, halfway along the left hand side of the left stitch.

4 Take the needle from right to left under all three stitches. Do not go through the fabric.

5 Pull the thread firmly. Take a second stitch from right to left under the vertical stitches.

6 Pull the thread through. Take the needle to the back very close to A. **Completed sheaf filling stitch.**

SHISHA STITCH

Shisha stitch is a traditional Indian technique for attaching tiny round pieces of mirror or tin to fabric background. There are numerous forms of Shisha stitch. Here we show one form. We used two colours of thread for photographic purposes only.

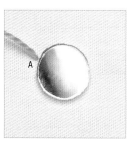

1 Framework. Bring the thread to the front at A approximately a third of the way down the left side.

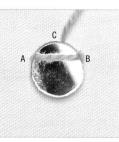

2 Take the thread to the back at B next to the edge of the glass, opposite A. Re-emerge at C, slightly above. Pull the thread through.

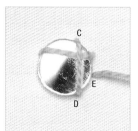

3 Take the thread to the back at D, below and directly opposite C. Re-emerge at E. Pull the thread through.

4 Take the thread to the back at F, on the opposite side. Re-emerge at G. Pull the thread through.

5 Take the thread to the back at H and re-emerge at I, just to the right of H. Pull the thread through.

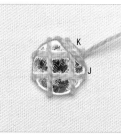

6 Take the thread to the back at J and re-emerge at K. Pull the thread through.

7 Take the thread to the back at L and re-emerge at M. Pull the thread through.

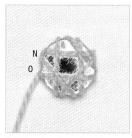

8 Take the thread to the back at N and re-emerge at O. Pull the thread through.

9 Take the thread to the back at P. Pull the thread through.
Completed foundation.

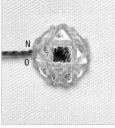

10 Edging stitches. Change to a new thread. Bring the thread to the front next to the glass on the left hand side between N and O.

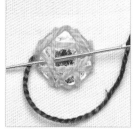

11 Loop the thread to the right and hold in place with your left thumb (thumb not shown). Take the needle under two crossed foundation stitches.

12 Ensure the loop is under the tip of the needle. Begin to pull the thread through.

13 Continue pulling until firm. Loop the thread to the left.

14 Take a small stitch parallel to the glass, close to the edge. Ensure the loop is under the tip of the needle.

15 Pull the thread through. **First completed edging stitch.**

16 Loop thread to the right and hold in place. Take the needle under the next two crossed foundation stitches. Ensure the loop is under tip of needle.

17 Pull the thread through until the loop is firm.

18 Loop thread to left. Take a small straight stitch parallel to edge of glass, taking the needle under the first stitch. Ensure loop is under tip of needle.

19 Pull the thread through until the loop is firm.

20 Loop the thread to the right. Take the needle under the next two crossed foundation stitches.

21 Pull the thread through. Loop the thread to the left. Take a small stitch through the previous stitch, picking up a small piece of fabric.

22 Continue working stitches in the same manner, turning the work as you proceed.

23 Take the last stitch into the back of the first stitch.

24 Completed shisha stitch.

SMOCKER'S KNOT

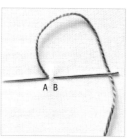 

A smocker's knot is firmer than a French knot.

In smocking and other embroidery, it is often used as a secure technique for finishing off on the back of the work. It can also be used as a decorative stitch.

1 Bring the thread to the front at A. Take a back stitch from B to A, keeping the thread above the needle.

2 Pull the thread through leaving a small loop approx 1cm (⅜") in diameter.

   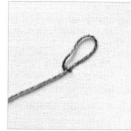

3 Take the needle through the loop.

4 Pull the thread through leaving a second small loop approx 1cm (⅜") in diameter.

5 Holding the thread in the left hand and the second loop in the right hand, begin to pull the second loop.

6 Pull until the first loop is tight and flat against the fabric. The second loop remains intact.

7 Take the needle through the remaining loop.

8 Begin to pull the thread through.

9 Pull the thread until a firm knot forms against the fabric.

10 Take the needle to the back under the knot to end off. **Completed smocker's knot.**

SPIDER WEB ROSE

This easy-to-stitch textured rose is created by weaving ribbon or thread through a framework of straight stitch spokes. Use an odd number of spokes. To begin and end off the ribbon, catch it to the stitching on the back of the work with sewing thread.

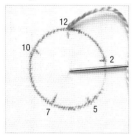

1 Draw a circle and mark points as shown. Using the thread, bring the needle to the front at the 12 o'clock mark. Take it to the back at the centre.

2 Work the stitches from the 5 o'clock mark and the 7 o'clock mark to the centre. Work the stitches from 10 o'clock and 2 o'clock in the same manner.

3 **Petals.** Bring the darkest shade of ribbon to the front between two spokes as close as possible to the centre.

4 Working in an anti-clockwise direction, weave the ribbon over and under the spokes of the framework until one round is complete.

5 Pull this round firmly so the threads of the framework do not show through the centre.

6 Weave a second round, allowing the ribbon to twist and loosening the tension slightly.

7 Take the needle to the back between two spokes, after weaving over a spoke. Pull the ribbon through. Cut off excess, leaving a 1cm (⅜") tail.

8 Using the medium shade of ribbon, emerge next to where the darkest ribbon went to the back.

9 Continue weaving, maintaining the over and under sequence for two more rounds. Take the ribbon to the back in the same manner as before.

10 Bring the lightest shade of ribbon to the front between the spokes just next to where the last ribbon was taken to the back.

11 Continue weaving until the framework is entirely hidden. Take the needle over one more spoke. Tuck it under the next spoke and take to the back.

12 Pull the ribbon through. On the wrong side, cut the ribbon. Secure any uncaught tails of the ribbon with the thread. **Completed spider web rose.**

SPLIT STITCH

Also known as Kensington outline stitch. Split stitch can be used as a line or as a filling.

Used extensively in the Middle Ages for embroidering faces, it lends itself to subtle shading when it is worked in multiple rows to fill a shape.

1 Draw a line on the fabric. Bring needle to front at A. Take the needle to the back at B approximately 3mm (⅛") away.

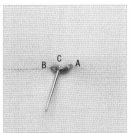

2 Pull the thread through. Emerge at C in the centre of the first stitch, splitting the thread with the needle.

3 Pull the thread through to complete the first stitch and begin the second stitch.

4 Take the needle to the back approximately 3mm (⅛") away.

5 Pull the thread through. Re-emerge through the centre of the second stitch.

6 Pull the thread through. Continue working stitches in the same manner. **Completed split stitch.**

SPLIT BACK STITCH

Unlike split stitch, the needle splits the thread of the previous stitch as it passes to the back of the fabric, rather than to the front.

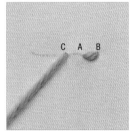

1 Draw a line on the fabric. Bring the needle to the front at A. Pull thread through. Take the needle to the back at B and re-emerge at C. Pull thread through.

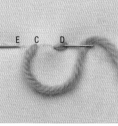

2 Take the needle to the back at D, splitting the threads of the previous stitch and re-emerging at E.

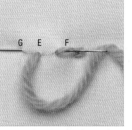

3 Pull the thread through. Take the needle from F to G splitting the second stitch as you take the needle to the back. Keep the stitches even in length.

4 Continue in the same manner to the end of the row. For the last stitch, take the needle to the back, splitting the previous stitch. End off.

SPRAT'S HEAD

Sprat's head is similar to crow's foot stitch.
This is traditionally a tailoring technique. It is used to strengthen a garment at a point of strain, for example, the top of a pleat. It can also be used decoratively to form a small triangular motif in an embroidery design.

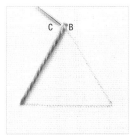

1 Draw a triangle the required size onto the fabric. Bring the thread to the front at A and take it to the back at B to form a straight stitch.

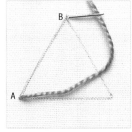

2 Pull the thread through and re-emerge at C, just to the left of B.

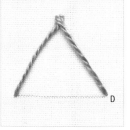

3 Pull the thread through. Take it to the back at D, at the remaining corner of the triangle.

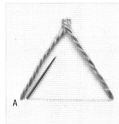

4 Pull the thread through and re-emerge just to the right of A.

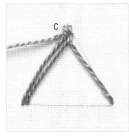

5 Take the needle to the back just below B on the drawn outline.

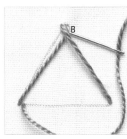

6 Pull the thread through. Emerge just below C on the drawn outline.

7 Pull thread through. Take the needle to the back on the line, just left of D. Pull through. Re-emerge at opposite end of line, just right of previous stitch.

8 Pull the thread through. Take the thread to the back on the right hand line just below the previous stitch. Pull the thread through.

9 Continue working stitches in the same manner, ensuring they overlap the previous stitches at the top.

10 Completely fill the shape. **Completed sprat's head.**

STAR STITCH

Star stitch is an isolated stitch, often worked to add interest and texture to a background. Contrasting colours and different weights of thread can be used to create various effects. It can be worked on canvas and even-weave fabrics as well as plain weave fabrics.

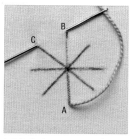

1 Mark the star onto the fabric. Bring the thread to the front at A. Take the needle from B to C.

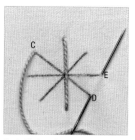

2 Pull the thread through. **Completed first stitch.** Take the needle from D to E. This stitch will lie over the first stitch.

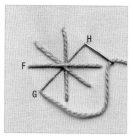

3 Pull the thread through. Take the needle from F to G and pull through. Take the needle to the back at H to form the final spoke of the star.

4 Bring the needle to the front near the centre, between two spokes. Take the needle over the intersection of the spokes and to the back, near the centre.

5 Pull the thread through to anchor the spokes at the centre. **Completed star stitch.**

6 A background of star stitches, formed with spokes of various lengths.

STEM STITCH

Also known as crewel stitch and South Kensington stitch. Stem stitch is similar in appearance to outline stitch. The thread is always kept below the needle, whereas in outline stitch it is kept above.

1 Draw a line on the fabric. Bring needle to front at left hand side of marked line. With thread below needle, take it to the back at A. Re-emerge at end of line.

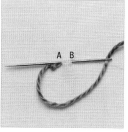

2 Pull the thread through. Again with the thread below the needle, take the needle from B to A.

3 Pull the thread through. Continue working the stitches in the same manner, always keeping the thread below the needle and the stitches the same size.

4 To end off, take the needle to the back for the last stitch but do not re-emerge. Secure the thread on the back with tiny back stitches. **Completed stem stitch.**

STEM STITCH – ENCROACHING

Encroaching stem stitch is a variation of stem stitch. The needle is angled across the line being stitched, rather than kept parallel to the line. This gives a wider looking stitch.

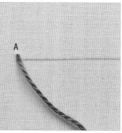

1 Draw a line on the fabric. Bring the thread to the front at A, slightly above the left hand end of the marked line. Lay the thread below the line.

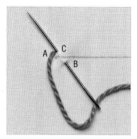

2 Take the needle from B, just below the line, to C which is next to A. The needle is angled across the line.

3 Pull the thread through. Take a second stitch from D, just below the line, to E which is directly above B.

4 Continue in the same manner to the end of the line. To end off, take the thread to the back on the line. This will 'square off' the end.

5 Completed encroaching stem stitch.

STEM STITCH – WHIPPED

This variation of stem stitch has a slightly more raised appearance. A foundation of stem stitch is worked first and then the whipping stitches are worked over this row.

1 Work a line of stem stitch to form the foundation for the whipping. End off. Secure a new thread on back of fabric. Bring to front just above the first stem stitch at the start of the line.

2 Take thread and needle over the stem stitch to the other side. Slide the needle in the space under the end of the first stitch and beginning of second stitch. Do not go through the fabric.

3 Pull thread through to form first whipped stitch. Again, take needle over line of stitching. Take it under the end of the second stitch and the beginning of the third stitch.

4 Continue in same manner to the end of the line. **Completed whipped stem stitch.**

STEM STITCH – PORTUGUESE KNOTTED

This delightful scroll-like stitch forms a knotted line which is useful for outlining shapes. Two whipping stitches are worked around each stem stitch creating a line of knots.

1 Work a stitch from A -B. Bring needle to front at C, on left of first stitch. With thread above needle, slide needle from right to left under stitch (below C).

2 Gently begin to pull the thread through.

3 Continue pulling the thread through. Pull upwards towards C, so a wrap is formed over the first stitch.

4 Keeping the thread above the needle, slide the needle under the first stitch again and below the first wrap.

5 Pull the thread through, so a second wrap is formed below the first.

6 To begin the second stem stitch, take the needle through to the back at D.

7 Pull the thread through.

8 Bring the needle to the front at B on the left hand side of the second stem stitch.

9 Keeping the thread above the needle, slide the needle from the right to the left under the first and second stem stitches (below B).

10 Pull the thread through. Keeping the thread above the needle, slide the needle from right to left under the wrap just formed.

11 Pull the thread through so a second wrap is formed.

12 Continue working stitches. To end off, take the needle to the back under the last wrap and finish off on the wrong side.

STEM STITCH – RAISED

Raised stem stitch is created from a base of straight stitches upon which rows of stem stitch are embroidered. It is best to work this stitch in a hoop, using a crewel needle for the base and a tapestry needle for the stem stitch.

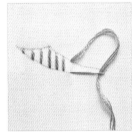

1 **Base.** Work evenly spaced parallel stitches at right angles to the shape outline and 2-3mm (⅛") apart. Start and finish the stitches exactly on the outline.

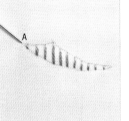

2 **Raised stem stitch.** Using a new thread, bring the needle to the front at A, on the left side of the shape.

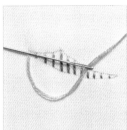

3 Pull through. Keeping thread below the needle, take the needle from right to left under first straight stitch. The needle does not go through the fabric.

4 Begin to gently pull the thread downwards.

5 Continue pulling until the stem stitch wraps firmly around the straight stitch. **Completed first raised stem stitch.**

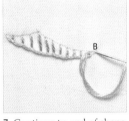

6 Take the needle from right to left under the next straight stitch. Holding it in place, pull thread through in the same manner as the first stitch.

7 Continue to end of shape. Slide needle behind straight stitches and pack the stem stitches down. Take needle to back at B, at point of shape.

wrong side of fabric

8 Pull through. Turn the work to the wrong side. Slide the needle under the straight stitches on the back of the work.

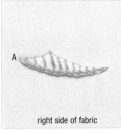

right side of fabric

9 Turn work to the right side. Re-emerge at A. Work a second row of raised stem stitch in the same manner. The rows of stitches will touch each other.

10 Continue working rows in the same manner. As the shape fills, start and finish rows away from tips of shape so they don't become too thick and bulky.

11 To achieve a clean, crisp look, ensure that the start and finish of each row is precisely on pencil line. Pack down each row before beginning the next.

12 Continue working rows of stem stitch until shape is filled and straight stitches are completely covered. Take thread to back on pencil line and end off.

STEM STITCH – RIBBON ROSE

The stitches are worked with a loose tension to keep the petals full. We used a no.24 chenille needle and 3 shades of 2mm (¹⁄₁₆") wide silk ribbon.

indicates top of fabric ↑

1 Using the darker shade of ribbon, work a French knot for the centre.

2 Inner petals. Change to medium shade. Bring the needle to the front at A alongside the knot.

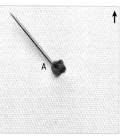

3 Pull the ribbon through. Take the needle to the back at B and re-emerge at C, keeping the ribbon below the needle.

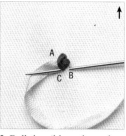

4 Pull the ribbon through. **Completed first stem stitch.**

5 Take the needle to the back at D and re-emerge at E, close to B, and pull through.

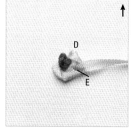

6 Rotate the fabric. Work a third stitch from E to F emerging at G.

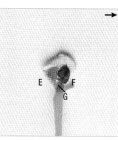

7 Rotate the fabric. Take the needle to the back at H, just beyond A and on the outside of the first stitch.

8 Pull the ribbon through. **Completed first round of petals.**

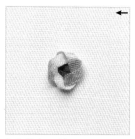

9 Outer petals. Change to lightest shade. Bring the needle to the front at I, halfway along and on the outside of the first stitch.

10 Pull the ribbon through. Rotate the fabric. Work a stitch from I to J, re-emerging at K.

11 Work four more stitches with the last stitch overlapping the first stitch of this round. Rotate the fabric as you work.

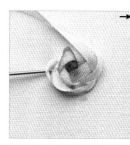

12 Pull ribbon through and end off on the back. **Completed stem stitch ribbon rose.**

STRAIGHT OVERCAST STITCH

Also known as overcast stitch. Straight overcast stitch is often featured in eyelets and cutwork. Here it is used to create a beading eyelet. The eyelet is first outlined with running stitch to reinforce the cut edge.

indicates top of fabric ↑

1 Mark a line on fabric. Care- fully outline the marked line for the eyelet with tiny running stitches starting on one side. Finish with thread on front.

2 Using small sharp-pointed scissors, carefully snip along the marked line.

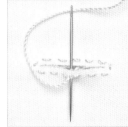

3 Take the needle to the back through the opening and re-emerge just beyond the running stitches to the right of the starting point.

4 Pull the thread through. Take the needle through the opening and re-emerge as close as possible to the first stitch on the right hand side.

5 Continue stitching in this manner along the side, keeping an even tension and ensuring the stitches are the same length.

6 At the end, slightly fan the stitches until the corner is completely turned.

7 Turn the fabric and continue stitching along the second side.

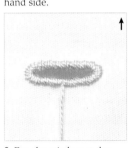

8 Fan the stitches at the second end in the same manner as before. Continue stitching until reaching the first stitch.

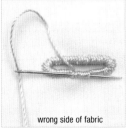

wrong side of fabric

9 To end off, take the needle through the opening to the back. Turn the fabric over to the wrong side. Slide the needle behind the stitches only.

wrong side of fabric

10 Take the needle over 1-2 threads, then slide the needle behind the stitches in the opposite direction.

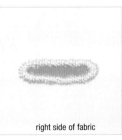

right side of fabric

11 Pull the thread taut and cut close to the stitches. **Completed straight overcast stitch eyelet.**

12 Ribbon threaded beading, created from straight overcast stitch eyelets.

STRAIGHT STITCH – FLOWER

Straight stitch can be used in a variety of ways and is often combined with other stitches. Here, straight stitches worked in a circle are used to form the petals of a flower.

1 Draw two circles on the fabric. Bring the thread to the front on the outer edge of the circle. Take it to the back on the inner circle.

2 Pull the thread through to complete the first straight stitch. Re-emerge on the outer edge opposite the first stitch. Take the needle to the back on the inner circle.

3 Continue working stitches, varying their length slightly and always working the stitches roughly opposite each other.

4 Continue until circles are filled. Add 3-7 colonial knots for the centre. **Completed straight stitch flower.**

Hints on working with ribbon

1 Use short lengths of ribbon approximately 30cm (12") long. Ribbon wears as it is pulled through the fabric and can quicklybecome frayed and worn.

2 Use a needle with a large eye – the larger the hole made in the fabric by the needle, the less wear there is on the ribbon.

3 Spread the ribbon by sliding the shaft of the needle along the underside of the ribbon while holding it taut.

4 Take stitches that are longer than the ribbon width so the ribbon has enough length to spread to its full width.

5 Work with a loose tension so the stitches remain full and do not lose their shape.

6 Leave a small tail of ribbon approximately 1cm (⅜") long on the back of the work when starting and ending. Secure the tails by stitching through them with other stitches or with fine embroidery thread. Knots on the back of the work leave lumps in the finished embroidery.

7 To prevent ribbon from twisting, place each stitch flat on the fabric and hold in place with your thumb while pulling the ribbon through.

8 If possible, stitch with your left fingers behind your work to carefully push the ribbon of previous work out of the way. This helps to prevent you from accidentally spearing the previous stitches with your needle and distorting them. Left handers stitch with their right hand behind the work.

Hints on lacing and framing an embroidery

1 Allow a minimum of 10cm(4") on all sides of the embroidery. This provides the framer with enough fabric to tension the work when framing.

2 Before lacing, ensure there are no dirty marks on your embroidery. Clean if necessary.

3 Ensure the embroidery is complete.

4 Never glue, staple or tape needlework as this can lead to deterioration of the fabric and threads.

5 Take your laced embroidery to a reputable framer, preferably one who has experience with embroidery.

6 Choose the mounts and frame to complement the colours in the embroidery.

STRAIGHT STITCH – RAISED

Raised straight stitch is worked in the same manner as straight stitch. To achieve the raised appearance of the stitch, place the needle under the stitches and carefully loosen them. In this example the stitch is used to create a daisy.

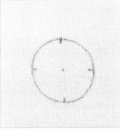

1 Mark a circle the size of the finished flower on the fabric. Mark the centre and then each quarter.

2 Bring the needle to the front at the centre and take it to the back at A, to form a loose straight stitch.

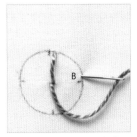

3 **Completed first stitch.** Bring the needle to the front at the centre and take it to the back at B, to form a second loose straight stitch.

4 **Completed second stitch.**

5 Bring the needle to the front 1-2mm (¹⁄₁₆") away from the centre to begin the third stitch. Take needle to the back at C, to form a loose straight stitch.

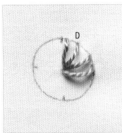

6 Work a fourth loose straight stitch to D, beginning just out from the centre as for the third stitch. **Completed third and fourth stitches.**

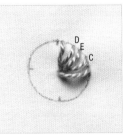

7 Work the fifth stitch (E) be- tween C and D, beginning at the centre. This completes the first quarter of the circle.

8 To raise the stitches, place the needle under them and gently lift. This ensures all the stitches are raised equally.

9 Work the second quarter in the same manner. Place the needle under the 5 completed stitches to raise them (refer to step 8). Ten stitches are now completed.

10 Repeat for the remaining 2 quarters. There are now 20 raised straight stitches. **Completed raised straight stitch petals.**

11 Work a French knot (1wrap) in the centre. **Completed daisy.**

12 **Pink daisies worked using 6 strands of stranded cotton.**

STUMPWORK – RASPBERRY

Each raspberry is created from a dense mass of French and colonial knots which shade from dark to light from one side of the berry to the other. Using different sized knots gives texture and character to the berries. We used 4 shades of crewel wool and tiny glass beads.

1 Draw a circle slightly smaller in diameter than the desired size of the finished berry. Using darkest shade, work 4 French knots in one third of the circle.

2 Using the same colour yarn, scatter 2-4 colonial knots in the same area. Leave the yarn dangling.

3 Using a paler shade of yarn, stitch 6-8 French or colonial knots among those already worked. Leave the yarn dangling.

4 Using the next palest shade, work knots along the upper edge of this section, merging the three shades. The lower section is completely filled.

5 Using the same shade, dense-ly fill the middle third of the circle with French and colonial knots. Leave the yarn dangling.

6 With the lightest shade, work French and colonial knots in the remaining section of the circle. Leave the yarn dangling.

7 Re-thread the darkest shade and work 5-6 knots on top of those already worked in the first third of the circle. Leave the yarn dangling.

8 Re-thread the second shade and work knots in the first third of the circle and merge into the middle of the circle. Leave the yarn dangling.

9 Re-thread the third shade and continue working knots over those already stitched, merging from the middle third to the last third. Leave the yarn dangling.

10 Finally, re-thread the lightest shade in the berry and work French and colonial knots in the last section of the circle.

11 To smooth the edges, work knots in any gaps around the edge. Use the shade that matches the adjacent knots. End off the yarns on the back.

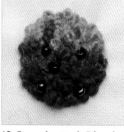

12 Securely attach 5 beads using doubled sewing thread. Pull the thread firmly so beads nestle among the knots. **Completed raspberry.**

TÊTE DE BOEUF STITCH (BULL'S HEAD STITCH)

A filling stitch, tête de boeuf produces an attractive pattern and can be used on a variety of fabrics. It can be worked with any type of thread, but the stitches stand out most effectively if a round thread such as perle cotton is used.

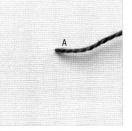

1 Secure the thread on the back of the fabric. Bring the thread to the front at A.

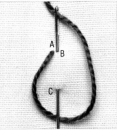

2 Insert the needle at B, as close as possible to A, and re-emerge at C. Loop the thread under the tip of the needle.

3 Pull the thread through to tighten the loop. Take thexneedle to the back at D, just below C, to anchor the loop.

4 Bring the needle to the front at E. Pull the thread through. Take the needle to the back at F.

5 Pull the thread through. Re-emerge at G and take the needle to the back at H.

6 Pull the thread through. **Completed tête de boeuf stitch.**

THORN STITCH

A decorative form of couching, thorn stitch makes a wide branching line which can be used to depict ferns, stems and grasses. If a heavy thread is used for the foundation stitch and a finer thread for the diagonal stitches, the effect is textured and fern-like. It is best worked in a hoop.

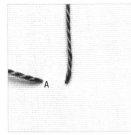

1 Work a long straight stitch for the foundation. Bring the thread to the front at A, a short distance left of the lower end of the foundation stitch.

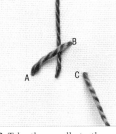

2 Take the needle to the back at B, just crossing, and very close to the foundation stitch. Pull thread through and re-emerge at C, directly opposite A.

3 Take the needle to the back at D, directly opposite B. Pull the thread through. Re-emerge at E to begin the second pair of diagonal stitches.

4 Continue working stitches in the same manner. **Completed thorn stitch.**

THREAD PAINTING

Thread painting creates a natural looking object; one that is 'painted' with thread. Each row is worked with stitches of random length, unlike conventional long and short stitch where only the first row is of uneven length. We used 2 strands of stranded cotton and a no.10 crewel needle.

1 The peach is worked in 5 shades, the leaves 3 shades of green and the stem, 1 shade of light brown. Draw design onto fabric. Stitch the outlines in back stitch or split stitch.

2 **Peach.** Starting from an outlined edge, work long and short stitch in the darkest shade. Vary the length of the stitches and ensure that they just cover the outlines.

3 Graduating from the darker to the lighter shades, continue filling the shape in long and short stitch.

4 Complete the peach using the lightest shade for the highlights.
Leaves. Using the palest green, work centre vein in stem stitch.

5 Fill in the leaves with satin stitch, completing one side before stitching the next. The darkest green is used close to the peach.

6 **Stem.** Using the light brown thread and starting from the base, work the stem in satin stitch.
Completed peach.

Hints on Thread Painting

1 When choosing colours, use as many shades as you can, even if they are similar. The result is more realistic. Try blending shades in the needle to create new colours.

2 Work well into the previous row of stitches to achieve a smooth blend. Avoid finishing at the end of a previous row, as this will create a visible line.

3 Keep the stitch length as random as possible. This will help to blend the colours and create a smooth surface.

4 Angle your needle into the fabric rather than pushing it straight through. This helps to blend the stitches.

5 Study the object carefully. In the case of fruit, stitches should run from base to stem rather than across the piece of fruit. For leaves, the stitches should run in the same direction as veins on a real leaf.

6 Observing your work from a distance will help you to be more critical and will show up any problems not visible when viewed closely.

TWIRLED RIBBON ROSE

The special effect of a twirled ribbon rose is achieved by twisting the ribbon tightly as the rose is formed. The result is a firmly wound, soft ribbon rose.

We used 4mm (³⁄₁₆") wide silk ribbon. Cut short lengths (no longer than 20cm- 8") so the ribbon does not become worn. Prepare a needle threaded with matching sewing thread. In this illustration we used contrasting thread for photographic purposes only.

1 Secure the ribbon on the back of the work. Bring it to the front at the position for the centre of the rose (A).

2 Hold the needle up so that the ribbon is vertical to the fabric. Begin to twist the needle in an anti-clockwise direction.

3 Continue twirling the needle until the ribbon is tightly twisted. Stop when the ribbon begins to buckle.

4 Using your thumb and fore-finger, grasp the coiled ribbon approximately 3cm (1¼") from the fabric.

5 Still holding on, and keeping the ribbon taut, fold it over to form a loop.

6 Hold the two parts of the ribbon close to A. Release the looped end. The ribbon will twist around itself forming a double coil.

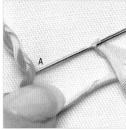

7 Still holding the double coil, take the needle to the back of the fabric just next to A.

8 Pull the ribbon through until reaching the doubled coil. Continue pulling gently until the rose is the desired size.

9 Using the thread, secure with two tiny stitches through the ribbon near the centre. Place the stitches as invisibly as possible.

10 **Completed twirled ribbon rose.**

WHEATEAR STITCH

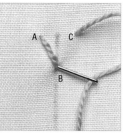 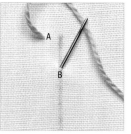 

This stitch is usually worked in straight lines and often in short segments. It is worked down a line towards you. The appearance of the stitch can be varied by altering the placement and length of the straight stitch 'ears'. Rule a vertical line on the fabric to help with stitch placement.

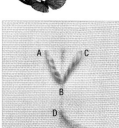

1 Bring the thread to the front at A to the left of the line. Take the needle to the back at B, on the line below and to the right of A.

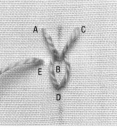

2 Pull the thread through. Re-emerge at C directly opposite A. Take needle to the back at B.

3 Pull the thread through. Re-emerge at D directly below B on the marked line.

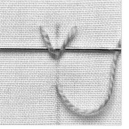

4 Slide the needle from right to left behind the previous two stitches. Do not pierce the fabric.

5 Take the needle to the back at D using the same hole in the fabric. Pull thread through and re-emerge at E on the left hand side (below A and opposite B).

6 Continue working stitches down the line in the same manner. **Completed wheatear stitch.**

WHIPPING STITCH

Whipping is a combination stitch where a second thread is worked over a foundation line of another stitch. It can be worked over a multitude of stitches, but here it is worked over a couched thread.

1 Work a line of couched thread to cover the design line. Secure a new thread on the back. Bring it to the front, just to the left of the foundation stitching.

2 Taking the needle from right to left, slide the eye under the second segment of laid thread. Do not pierce the fabric.

3 Pull the thread through gently. Slide the eye of the needle from right to left under the third segment.

4 Pull the thread through. Continue working in the same manner to the end of the line. **Completed whipping.**

WHIPPED STITCH ROSE

Worked in three shades of 7mm (⁵⁄₁₆") ribbon, this beautiful rose is created from a French knot surrounded by three rounds of whipped stitches. Use a no.18 chenille needle and turn the fabric as you work.

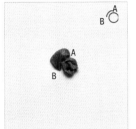

1 Using the darkest shade, work a loose French knot in the centre. **First round.** Using the same ribbon, work a straight stitch from A to B.

2 Bring the needle to the front just below and to the left of A.

3 Take the needle over the straight stitch and then under it. The needle does not go through the fabric.

4 Pull the ribbon through, ensuring it loosely wraps around the straight stitch but does not twist.

5 Work a second loose wrap in same manner near B. Work a third wrap over the centre. Take needle to back under straight stitch halfway between A and B.

6 Pull the ribbon through forming another loose wrap over the centre. **Completed first whipped stitch.**

7 Following steps 1-6, work three more whipped stitches in the same manner. End off the ribbon on the back. **Completed first round.**

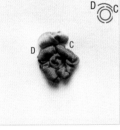

8 **Second round.** Using a paler shade of ribbon, work a whipped stitch from C to D.

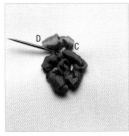

9 Bring the needle to the front at E, just between D and the first round of stitches.

10 Work a second whipped stitch from E to F in the same manner.

11 Work three more whipped stitches, slightly overlapping each with the previous stitch. End off the ribbon on the back **Completed second round.**

12 **Third round.** Using the palest shade, work a third round of seven whipped stitches in the same manner. End off. **Completed whipped stitch rose.**

WOOL ROSE

Beautiful roses are created quickly and easily by using tapestry wool. Select a darker colour for the centre and a lighter shade for the surrounding satin stitch petals. You can use either a chenille or tapestry needle, depending on the fabric. The size is dependent on the thickness of the wool.

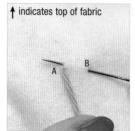

↑ indicates top of fabric

1 Bring the wool to the front at A. Take the needle to the back at B and bring it to the front 1-2 fabric threads above A. The needle is slightly angled.

2 Pull wool through to make first stitch. Take second stitch by placing needle directly opposite the emerging thread and angling the needle as shown.

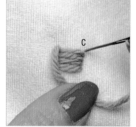

3 Work another 2 stitches (there are now 4). To complete the 5th stitch forming the square, take the needle to the back at C, opposite emerging thread.

4 **Completing the centre square.** Bring the needle up at D (top left of square) using the same hole as the previous stitch.

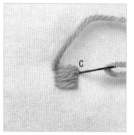

5 Take the needle to the back at C (use the same hole). Do not pull too tight. The wool should lie snugly over the previous stitch.

6 Bring the needle up just below D (using the same hole as the stitch in the previous layer).

7 Take the needle to the back just below C. Bring it to the front just below emerging thread.

8 Continue working in the same manner. After placing the 4th stitch, and to complete the 5th, take the needle through to the back in the lower right corner.

9 You should now have a padded square.

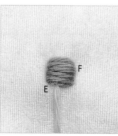

10 **First petal (E-F).** Change to a lighter shade. Knot the end. Bring the needle up at the left of the centre (E) below the padded square.

11 Take the needle to the back at F, approximately level with the second stitch of padding.

12 Re-emerge just to the right of E.

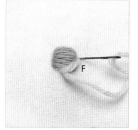

13 Take the needle to the back slightly higher and wider than F.

14 Settle the stitch with the thumb. Note how it snuggles around the first stitch of the petal.

15 Bring the wool to the front just to the right of E again. Shape the thread around for the final stitch.

16 Take the needle to the back slightly higher and wider than the previous stitch.

17 Settle the final stitch to snugly curve around the outer edge of the petal. **Finished petal E-F.**

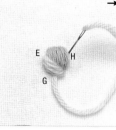

18 Second petal (G-H). Rotate the fabric. Bring the needle up at G (left of the centre). Take the needle to the back at H, level with the first stitch (E).

19 Finished first stitch of petal G-H.

20 Follow steps 12-17 to com-plete the petal. **Finished second petal** (this makes a lovely bud).

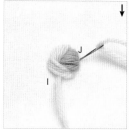

21 Third petal (I-J). Rotate the fabric. Bring the needle up at I and take to the back at J.

22 Follow steps 12-17 to complete the petal. **Finished third petal.**

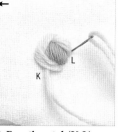

23 Fourth petal (K-L). Rotate the fabric. Bring the needle up at K and take to the back at L.

24 Follow steps 12-17 to complete the petal. Press firmly with the thumb to 'settle' the rose. **Finished rose.**

WOUND ROSE

This elegant wound ribbon rose is made from a 50cm (20") length of 7mm (⁵⁄₁₆") silk ribbon. A spare needle is inserted into the fabric to form the framework around which the ribbon is wound. After the ribbon is wound, couch it in place to secure it to the fabric.

1 Take a spare needle through the fabric for approx 3mm (⅛"). Bring the ribbon to the front just above where the spare needle entered the fabric.

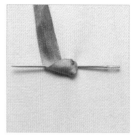

2 Wrap the ribbon in a clockwise direction over the needle and then under the tip of the needle.

3 Wrap ribbon in an anti-clockwise direction over the needle and under the needle eye (forming a figure 8). Pack ribbon towards centre of spare needle.

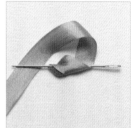

4 Put one fold in ribbon. Take ribbon behind tip of needle in an anti-clockwise direction. The fold is on right hand side. Keep ribbon loose so it lies flat.

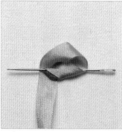

5 Gently slide the ribbon towards the centre of the needle so the rose will become round in shape rather than oval.

6 Continue winding the ribbon in an anti-clockwise direction and putting one fold in each side until the rose is the required size (approx 3-4 rounds).

7 Take the ribbon to the back under one end of the spare needle. Leave it dangling on the back of the work.

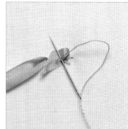

8 **Wrong side of work.** Using matching machine sewing thread, secure the beginning of the ribbon on the back of the fabric.

9 Bring the thread to the front near a fold in the centre circle of ribbon. Work a tiny straight stitch to hold the fold in place.

10 Continue working tiny straight stitches at the folds in the ribbon. Remove spare needle and anchor wraps of ribbon at each end of the centre wrap.

11 End off the thread. Bring ribbon to front and work three overlapping straight stitches on the lower part of the rose.

12 Work 3-4 more overlapping straight stitches under the first row to fill out the flower.
Completed wound rose.

WOVEN FILLING STITCH

Also known as Queen Anne stitch. This is a darning stitch created from parallel straight stitches through which the thread is woven. The parallel vertical stitches covering the entire shape, form the framework for the weaving.

1 **Framework.** Bring the thread to the front at A. Take to the back at B to form a long straight stitch.

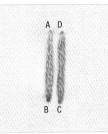

2 Re-emerge at C and take a second long straight stitch to D.

3 Work more straight stitches over the shape in the same manner to form the framework.

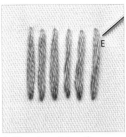

4 **Weaving.** Bring the needle to the front at E, just to the right of the last vertical stitch and very close to the top of it.

5 Weave the needle over the last vertical stitch and under the stitch next to it. Hint: you may find it easier to weave with the needle eye.

6 Continue weaving over and under the stitches.

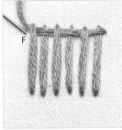

7 Take the needle to the back of the fabric at F, just to the left of the first vertical stitch and level with the line of weaving.

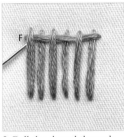

8 Pull the thread through. Bring the needle to the front just below F.

9 Pull the thread through. Weave to the other side – over, under, over, under, over, under.

10 Take the needle to the back at G. Pull the thread through and re-emerge just below this point.

11 Continue weaving from side to side until the vertical stitches are completely covered. **Completed shape.**

12 **Woven filling stitch is worked to form the basket of this topiary.**

ZIGZAG STITCH

Zigzag stitch can be used as a counted thread or surface embroidery stitch. Pretty geometric patterns in zigzag are often used for outlines or borders.

Worked in multiple rows, it is effective for filling a shape. When used as a filling stitch, the vertical rows should touch. Ruling parallel lines will help to keep your stitches even when not working on evenweave fabric.

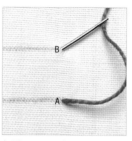

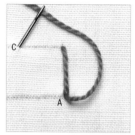

1 **First step.** Secure thread on back. Bring thread to front at A on lower line. Take the needle to the back at B on the upper line directly above A.

2 Pull thread through to form a vertical straight stitch. Re-emerge at A (through same hole). Take the needle to the back at C on the upper line.

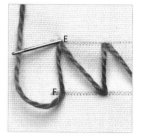

3 Pull thread through to form a diagonal straight stitch. Re-emerge at D on lower line directly below C. Insert the needle at C (through same hole).

4 Pull the thread through. Re-emerge at D (through the same hole). Take needle to back at E on upper line (same distance as B and C).

5 Pull thread through. Bring the needle to the front at F directly below E. Work a straight stitch from F to E.

6 **Second step.** Re-emerge at F and insert the needle at E. This will form a second straight stitch between F and E.

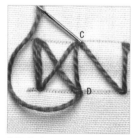

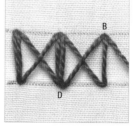

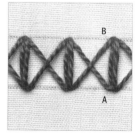

7 Re-emerge at F again. Take the needle to the back at C (through the same hole).

8 Pull the thread through. Re-emerge at D (through the same hole). Take the needle to the back at C and pull through.

9 Re-emerge at D again. Take the needle to the back at B and pull through.

10 Re-emerge at A. Take the needle to the back at B to work a straight stitch from A to B. **Completed zigzag stitch.**

Index